Help! I'm a Newlywed...

What Do I Do Now?

WIFE-SAVING ADVICE

EVERY NEW BRIDE MUST KNOW

TO SURVIVE THE FIRST YEAR OF MARRIAGE

Help! I'm a Newlywed...

What Do I Do Now?

☙

Wife-Saving Advice
Every New Bride Must Know
to Survive the First Year of Marriage

Lorraine Sanabria Robertson

30 Miles Media, Inc.
www.AskWifey.com

30 Miles Media, Inc.
P.O. Box 1216
Mableton, GA 30126
30MilesMedia@comcast.net
www.AskWifey.com

This book was written to provide information and to entertain. It is not meant to take the place of marital counseling, legal advice, financial advice or any other professional service. While thorough and efficient effort was made to insure accuracy, there may be typographical and/or content errors. The author and 30 Miles Media, Inc. have no responsibility or liability for any loss or damages claimed as a result of any information in this book.

Some names of the people quoted in this book have been changed to protect their privacy.

Publisher's Cataloging-in-Publication (Provided by Quality Books, Inc.)

    Robertson, Lorraine Sanabria.
      Help! I'm a newlywed-- what do I do now? :
    wife-saving advice every new bride must know to survive
    the first year of marriage / Lorraine Sanabria
    Robertson. -- 1st ed.
      p. cm.
    LCCN 2007903351
    ISBN-13: 978-0-9796459-3-8
    ISBN-10: 0-9796459-3-X

      1. Marriage—Handbooks, manuals, etc. 2. Wives—Life
    skills guides. 3. Newlyweds—Life skills guides.
    4. Man-woman relationships.   I. Title.

    HQ734.R63 2008   306.81
                QBI07-700132

First Edition

Cover Design by Goldfinger c.s.
Book Design by Leila Joiner
Author Photograph by gr8photo.com

For Napoleon,

My favorite husband in the whole wide world!

Contents

Acknowledgments

Wow! I did it! Napoleon — you were right. Thank you for being the best husband ever. Your love, encouragement, support and ability to push me farther than I thought I could ever go are priceless. Thank you for being you; and for letting me put it in a book. To my little pookie-doodles, Miles and Milan, thank you for understanding when Mommy needed five more minutes on the computer. Yes, we can go outside and play now.

To my mom, Marsha Sanabria, you believed in this project from the moment I screamed, "*Help!*" Thank you for your unconditional love and support and for daring me to dive into the pool — it feels great in here! To my dad, Mario Sanabria, you thought you got rid of me when you walked me down the aisle — not! You are always there when I need you, and always willing to help! Thank you for everything. To my sister, Nicole Sanabria, mi hermana and personal editor, thanks for always being there for me and my family, and for being the best sister, and friend, a girl could have. To my #1 G-ma, Joyce Wilson, you have always been there for me whenever I've needed anything — and you came through again on this one. Thank you so much — #2 Granddaughter!

To Marlene and Leon Robertson, boy did I get lucky; not only did I marry the best husband, but I got the best in-laws, too! Thanks for raising such a wonderful man for me to marry; and for loving me like I was your own. To all of my family, the Sanabrias and Wilsons — there are way too many to name — many thanks for your love and support.

To my peoples — Lesa, Rick, Nancy, Noelle, Rob, Dana, Ron, Melanie, Rob, April, Chance, Cat, Rory, Jo, Wanda, Millian, Tammy, Chris, Lu, Sheilah, Michelle, Tashion and Sharliss — you know that book I've been writing forever?... well, it's finally done! Thanks for your support, friendship and good times!

To Lisa Cambridge, what a wonderful person and friend you are! You were so instrumental on so many levels in making sure this project came to fruition. You believed in me from the second I walked in your office at LaFace and have always been there for me since. Thanks for your friendship, your encouragement, and for kicking me in the butt when I needed it.

To D. L. Warfield, thanks for seeing my vision, creating Wifey, and producing such a fabulous book cover. To Robin Quinn, editor extraordinaire! Thanks for helping me make this book the best that it can be in so many ways. To Janine Coveney, I truly appreciate your copyediting expertise. To Leila Joiner, you were right on point with the interior design. Thanks for making my words look so good! To Jo Moore Stewart, what can I say, your creativity and generosity are inspiring. Thanks for constantly throwing new ideas at me, and yes, I am writing them down!

To Stephan and Joanne at Best Coaches, Inc., and my 90 Day Dream Team — you guys are awesome. Thanks for helping me just freakin' do it! It's a done deal, baby.

To Tina McElroy Ansa and everyone involved at the Sea Island Writer's Retreat, what a productive and positive weekend! Tina, thanks for sharing your passion, your knowledge and for checking in on me. As you can see, I am doing what writers do — writing!

To Dolly Turner, Carole Hall, LaJoyce Brookshire, Dawn Marie Daniels, Joyce Davis, Lloyd Jassin, Pamela Harty, Ndidi Massey, Courtney Barnes, Gil Robertson, Jamie Foster Brown (who published my first article), Renita Mathis and the many others who have been instrumental in my writing career. I appreciate your time, consideration and professional support!

To all the women who took the time to share their thoughts, feelings, experiences and advice with me and with the many new brides who will read this book, thank you! Please know that your input has touched somebody's life.

And most importantly, thanks to God for blessing me with something meaningful to say, the talent to write it down, and the courage to get out of my own way and make it happen.

Love & Smiles,

Lorraine

Help! I'm a Newlywed...

What Do I Do Now?

Why I Wrote This Book

HELP! I'M A NEWLYWED... WHAT DO I DO NOW? That's a thought most new wives have at some time — in the kitchen, or the bedroom, when the in-laws come to visit, or maybe during everyday conversation with your husband. Regardless of where or why you thought it — you did! And if you're anything like me, you were probably too scared to ask anyone what you should do. That's exactly why I wrote *Help! I'm a Newlywed... What Do I Do Now? Wife-Saving Advice Every New Bride Must Know to Survive the First Year of Marriage.*

As a former glowing bride, I found my wedding day to be the happiest, most magical day of my life. I married my best friend, Napoleon, a man I had been involved with for more than five years and was engaged to for one. I was ecstatic that I found the man I wanted to start a family with, to travel around the world with, and to share denture cream with once we're old and gray. My face beamed brightly all day, and I have very expensive pictures to prove it. I was absolutely certain that I had made the right decision — I love this man madly — so why was I about to go crazy?

I must've read every bridal magazine in existence during my engagement. They were very informative about everything leading up to my wedding. The problem was that very little information was available about what to do when I got back from my tropical-paradise honeymoon. Not much for when we walked through the door as husband and wife and had to live with each other — and like it! There was no one saying, "*It's going to be an adjustment,*" or "*It's OK not to know what to do now.*" All I heard was "*You must be so happy*" or "*You're so lucky to be married.*" Now don't get me wrong, I was happy, but I was also terrified of my new role in my relationship!

One day, I finally got up the nerve to ask my mother why Napoleon and I were fighting more than usual. And then I asked my aunt why I had to cook dinner every night. And what was I supposed to cook? I even asked my girlfriend how to get my husband to pick up his dirty clothes after he steps out of them each day.

After opening my mouth and screaming, "*Help! I'm a newlywed... what do I do now?*" I found out that I wasn't alone. And most important, that I was perfectly normal. I discovered that millions of women and men have millions of questions about being married and that doesn't mean they don't love their spouses or don't like being married. It just means they need help. So here it is...help...to hopefully make things a little easier for you and your new hubby.

Now I must tell you that I am not a doctor, a counselor or a therapist. I have not completed years of scientific research, nor do I plan to bore you, or myself, with any. I'm a wife. Correction, I'm a happy, loving, sometimes frightened, confused and frustrated but willing-to-learn, madly-in-love-with-my-spouse, still-figuring-things-out wife — just like you. I've successfully survived the newlywed years — my husband and I are celebrating eight exciting years together — and we continue to work hard to make our marriage work.

Now some of the advice in this book is first-hand, about things that I've done and some are things I wish that I did. I've drawn from my own ongoing experiences in this exciting world of marriage and I thought it would be helpful to share all of this with you. Plus, I've talked to countless brides and wives — newly engaged, freshly married and old-school veterans — and have taken into account their stories, joys and fears. I've asked for advice and suggestions from women and men of all ages, and I welcome yours, too.

My goal is to help new wives (and husbands, too) through the kinks of their happy but also scary new unions by offering suggestions for the many challenges and situations that they may face during the beginning of marriage. Hearing that other people were going through some of the same, very real adjustments of marriage that Napoleon and I were going through — no matter how large, small or silly they seemed — left me comforted and more confident in our relationship. I hope it will for you, too.

However, it's very important for you as a new wife to understand that every individual and couple is different. Some people face different obstacles than others and some handle the same obstacles in different ways. It is crucial to your relationship that you as a couple handle the challenges that you face in your marriage in ways that make you both comfortable and happy.

The Do's and Don'ts in this book are suggestions that I and many other newlyweds have found to be helpful. Some you may agree with, and some you may not. That's perfectly OK! *Do* take this book seriously and take all the advice that suits you, but also take it with a grain of salt and a sense of humor. And, most importantly, *don't* take anyone's advice (even mine) if you are not comfortable with it!

I love my husband, I love being married — and I'd love to keep it that way. In writing this book, I'm not only trying to help you, but to help myself, too. There's nothing wrong with not knowing what to do in your marriage, but there is something wrong with not finding out!

Happy Marriage & Best Wishes,

Wifey

1

After the Wedding

ONCE THE BOUQUET'S BEEN THROWN, THE GUESTS GO HOME, AND WEDDING WITHDRAWAL SETS IN

The wedding cake was served and eaten, the champagne popped and sipped, the dance floor rocked and cleared, and the guests have all gone home. Now it's just the two of you — you and your husband — alone together. Gulp! What do you do now? So many brides, myself included, spend so much of their time planning their special day that they forget one very important thing — there's life after the wedding!

After the presents have all been opened and you've been home a little while since your honeymoon, you may begin to realize that things are not quite the way that you expected them to be. If I had a dollar for every time a new bride told me that, I wouldn't need to win the Lotto — I could fund it! You are not alone if you feel this way! In fact, you are completely normal and in the same company as millions of other new brides.

It's so easy to let your expectations get the best of you. Your wedding day is sacred, a day that you've probably looked forward to your entire life. That kind of excitement and anticipation brings big expectations — but not ones that are very realistic.

I expected to return from my Mexican honeymoon and float in marital bliss for at least the first year with nothing to do but love my husband and have really great sex. Yeah, right. It sounded good. Then reality set in and I found out that there is more to marriage than love and sex — even really great sex! I didn't expect many of the relationship changes that happened — like adjusting to living together and dealing with our new extended families (we'll conquer those topics later in the book), and I definitely didn't expect to still be busy with so many post-wedding details.

Most of us don't think about all the work we still have to do after the wedding, like writing "thank you" notes, changing your name, and getting your dress cleaned. I was physically and mentally exhausted after my wedding day. I didn't expect to come home after the honeymoon and still have to deal with wedding drama. After all, my big day was over!

I also didn't expect to have wedding withdrawal. I was thrilled that my wedding day seemed flawless. It turned out one hundred times better than I imagined. Then I spent a week relaxing at a luxurious five-star hotel on the beach in Mexico with my new husband rubbing suntan oil all over my bronzed body. Yup, married life was looking and feeling pretty good at that point, until I got home and...*wham!*... wedding withdrawal came crashing out of nowhere like a big blue tidal wave and wiped out my picture-perfect fantasy.

What is wedding withdrawal? It's when you miss the fun,

excitement, anticipation, craziness and stress of planning your wedding. You've lived and breathed your wedding for probably most of your life — or at least the past six months. It's only natural to miss this. Wedding withdrawal can happen to the compulsive organizer or the carefree planner. Whether you had a five-course meal with 300 guests or an intimate dinner with immediate family and friends, planning your wedding can be as taxing as having a second full-time job.

Your wedding consumes so much of your mind and your time, then all of the sudden in one day you're done. It's over. Your wedding day has come and gone. No more appointments with the caterer. No more flowers to choose or pretty silk ribbons to tie around tiny bottles of bubbles. No more fantasizing about what your wedding day will be like, and the hardest part of wedding withdrawal: nothing for you to do.

But as I mentioned earlier, that's not entirely true, you do have things to do — lots of things to do — it just feels like you don't. And truthfully, the post-wedding wrap-up is not nearly as exciting as planning the wedding. Yes, you miss the planning, but writing out a million "thank you" notes and drafting letters to change your name are not exactly what you had in mind to take its place.

There's a void that comes after you've spent several months of your life living and breathing your wedding. You would think that any sane person would welcome wedding withdrawal and a much-needed break, but no, that would be too easy and not a likely thing for a new bride to do.

OK, so the fact is that most of us go through some sort of wedding planning withdrawal — whether it's missing the excitement of attending your first bridal expo, or the joy of thumbing through stacks of bridal magazines, or some other aspect of planning the biggest event of your life. And, let's be honest, many of us miss truly being the center of attention. It's the one day in your life when everything is all about you! Missing that is normal as long as you keep it in perspective.

Pay attention to your feelings, talk about them with your husband, and then let them go! You have something new and exciting to focus on now — your marriage! Sometimes it's easy to forget this, but that's really what the wedding is all about, not the music, nor the flowers, nor the delicious little crab-cake hors d'oeuvres. You are entering a very impressionable time in your marriage — the beginning — and you don't want to start it off on the wrong foot, especially a selfish one!

Don't expect your husband to completely understand what you're going through. Wedding withdrawal is not a man thing! In fact, he's probably happy to have the love of his life back, and to lose the chart-seating maniac he just married.

If you're having trouble letting go, curl up with your husband and relive the day by watching your wedding video. If that doesn't work, watch it again. Face it, no one wants to see it 50 times except you two. Pop some popcorn and grab a bottle of bubbly and enjoy the show! You can also look at your wedding photos. Not only now, but throughout your marriage. They can be a wonderful reminder of your special day and are the perfect cure for the wedding-withdrawal blues.

So don't put away your wedding notebook yet; now is the perfect time to knock out those "thank you" notes, get your dressed cleaned, and do some paperwork! Besides, handling the after-wedding wrap-up tasks can help ease the pain of the wedding withdrawal blues. Think of it as a transition period to ease you gradually out of your intense and sometimes neurotic planning mode into the exciting and eventful world of marriage.

Don't Panic!

You're married now and that can be scarier than you've imagined. But don't worry, you *will* adjust and get through it just fine. When your hands start sweating, your heart starts racing so fast that it scares you, and you can feel the panic taking over your body, stop and take a deep breath. You've just entered one of the most fulfilling, joyous and stressful unions that you will ever be a part of. You will *need* to take a deep breath often!

You will also need to remember that you are not alone. Most newlywed couples feel scared, nervous, uncertain, or overwhelmed at some point during their first year. And if they say they don't, they're either lying or they are visiting — from another planet! It is perfectly normal to feel all of these things, but trust me, panicking will not help you or your husband as you try and figure out what the two of you just got yourselves into.

And you will try to figure out what you just got yourself into. One day, you'll look at him and think, "*I'm married now. How did this happen?*" And then your life will flash before your eyes. OK, maybe it won't be that dramatic, but seriously, as you both start to adjust there will be times when you ask yourself, "*How did I get here?*" When things seem like they are very unfamiliar and out of your control, that's when panic comes creepin' around the corner. Don't let it get you! Take that deep breath, and tell yourself these three things:

1. I married my husband because we love and respect each other.
2. It's perfectly normal to be scared. What I'm feeling is normal.
3. We will figure things out together with communication and compromise.

Now, don't you feel better? Remind yourself of those three things as often as the need arises. This is just the beginning and you have a lot of work to do. Panicking will not solve anything. We'll tackle more on the newlywed jitters and keeping your cool in the next chapter, so for now focus on getting through your after-the-wedding tasks. It's OK that you don't have all of the answers; no one does when they first get married. You're not missing anything. No couple is given a map to the perfect marriage, because there is none! You and your husband will create it along the way.

Don't Expect Too Much

Expectations are like playing with a book of matches. You can strike one and light a sweet smelling candle, or you can strike one and burn the whole house down. Unless you already have fire insurance, put the matches and the expectations down.

Or you can talk about them honestly. They lose some of their spark if you and your husband share some of the things that you both expect to happen. Napoleon expected me to fold his shirts a certain way when we got married, and I expected him to wash and fold them himself. I expected Napoleon to tell me all of the sweet things he did before we got married and he expected not to have to repeat himself. This is where the fun begins.

I hope that you and your husband took the time to discuss some of your expectations before you got married. Most people tackle the big topics like how many kids you want to have, but they don't tell each other, "*I expect you to lock the doors every night*" or "*I expect you to buy my socks for me now that we're married.*" Yes, I inherited most of the shopping duties once I became the "Mrs." Who would have thought that buying socks would be something he expected me to do? Not me, and that's why you have to tell each other your expectations.

You each bring preconceived notions to your marriage. Make sure you talk about them so that you both are on the same page. If you don't, it will be extremely difficult for the two of you to fall into sync with one another. Being in sync in a marriage is a very important thing. You do not always have to agree with each other or do things the way the other likes, but if you are aware of each other's wants and expectations, you can figure out how to make everybody happy, and thus fall into sync. The only way to do that is to talk to each other. Neither one of you can read minds, so make sure to tell him what is on yours.

There's one more thing about expectations that you have to remember: just because you expect it doesn't mean it will happen. Just because you tell him that you expect it, still doesn't mean it will happen. It just means that you did the right thing and told him. Now you have to work together so that you both can figure out a way to get what you want. You can expect that won't always be easy.

Do Take the Time to Enjoy All of the Attention

Everyone showers newlyweds with attention. Eat it up and enjoy it! This is one of the best parts of being a newlywed. It's OK, you can admit it. You like being the center of attention for a while longer. People who love you are genuinely excited for you and people who barely know you are suddenly your best friend. Even the people who don't like you can't help but throw a little attention your way.

Bask in it. There's no other time that you get to be a Princess for a Day and let everyone fuss over you. Just don't be surprised when the attention ends. Like all good things, the fat lady sings and all of "your" attention is being heaped onto the next bride. Pick up your ego — and your diamond-studded tiara — and get over it! There is nothing more unattractive than a pouting new bride.

But while the attention is still flowing in, ride the wave and get the most out of it by trying a few of these ideas:

1. SHARE WEDDING DETAILS WITH PEOPLE WHO STILL WANT TO HEAR THEM. The little old lady who took my new driver's license picture at the Department of Motor Vehicles wanted to hear every detail. The line behind me was flaming mad, but I told her every joyous moment I could before they threatened to drag me off.

2. SHOW PEOPLE YOUR PICTURES. If you're like me, you almost needed a second mortgage on your home to pay for your wedding pictures. Napoleon and I vow that if our house is on fire, we're not leaving without our wed-

ding book! Get your money's worth by carrying a few special photos with you and show them to the attention-givers who are interested.

3. TALK TO NEWLY ENGAGED WOMEN. It wasn't that long ago that you were one of them, and if you remember correctly, the wedding seemed to be all you wanted to talk about. New brides are an eager and willing audience. Most of them want to hear and compare the smallest details. Take full advantage of this audience. They look up to you. You survived your wedding and are now considered an expert in their eyes. They have no clue that you have no clue either.

Do Send Out Your Thank You Notes In a Timely Manner

At many weddings, the bride and the groom often receive lots of cash and a mountain of fabulous gifts. Aside from gaining a gorgeous husband, this is one of the best perks of getting married. People buy you lots of wedding gifts that you get to pick out — even if they don't show up to the wedding. However, there is one catch... you have to write out a ton of "thank you" notes to make sure everyone knows how much you appreciate them. And you have to get them done within two weeks after the wedding. OK, two weeks is ideal, but if you are taking a honeymoon that might be unrealistic. It is fine to take a little more time, but don't let it drag out past three months.

Tearing through all those packages normally tops the list of fun things to do after the wedding, but sitting down to write out the "thank you" notes is a task that is often avoided. It doesn't have to be such a chore. Fill up the new crystal champagne flutes you just unwrapped, grab a pen, and get to writing. Here are a few tips to make it a little less painful:

1. HANDWRITE YOUR "THANK YOU" NOTES. Everything is computerized these days, but your "thank you" notes shouldn't be. You can get away with printing your labels, but the notes inside should be handwritten.

2. DON'T DISCUSS DOLLAR AMOUNTS. It's tacky, tacky, tacky. Instead, thank them for their *"generous gift."*

3. MENTION WHAT THE GIFT IS AND HOW YOU WILL USE IT. *"We love the beautiful Tiffany vase; it will look great in our new dining room."*

4. MAKE SURE TO SAY "WE" INSTEAD OF "I." You are married now, remember? The gifts were given to both of you. *"We were so delighted to receive our new coffee-maker. It will help us start our mornings off right!"*

5. SEND OUT NOTES TO THE PEOPLE THAT YOU KNOW ARE WAITING FOR THEM FIRST. If you know your mother's Aunt Betty keeps checking her mailbox, move her to the top of the list.

6. DON'T PANIC IF YOU RECEIVED A GIFT WITH NO CARD ATTACHED. IT HAPPENS. Most people will understand, and they will ask you if you received their gift if they never get a "thank you" card.

7. WRITE A GENERIC MESSAGE IF YOU'RE NOT SURE WHAT THE PERSON GAVE YOU. Sometimes gifts and

cards get mixed up. Don't sweat it; just thank them for such "*a wonderful gift*" and move on.

8. DON'T FORGET TO THANK YOUR VENDORS. If you were pleased with their service, send them a thank you note saying so. Much of their business thrives on recommendations and referrals, so take care of them the way they took care of you.

9. MAKE SURE TO KEEP YOUR LIST OF WHO GAVE YOU WHAT. You think you'll remember everything, but I promise, you won't. Then you can use that list when relatives or friends visit. Refer to your list, and then when your husband's Aunt Verna comes for the holidays, make sure you put out the yellow polka dot placemats that she gave you. Talk about earning brownie points!

10. AND, FINALLY, MAKE SURE TO MAKE WRITING THE NOTES FUN. For instance, you could write them out together. Light some candles, sip some wine, and when you're done, re-enact your wedding night.

Do Get Your Wedding Dress Cleaned and Preserved

It's probably the most expensive dress that you will ever buy, and it will probably be the most expensive cleaning bill you'll ever have — prices vary from around $100 and can easily climb past $500, depending on the size and details of the dress; and the city and state where you get it serviced. Bite the bullet — or in this case, the bill — and get it done. It sounds obvious, right? You buy a dress; you wear a dress; you clean a dress. You would be surprised how many brides skip this step and run the risk of their gorgeous white gown turning into a yellow-tinged rag.

With a few simple steps, you can ensure that your dress will stay in mint condition for you to squeeze back into on a special anniversary, to renew your vows, to pass on one day to your daughter, or just to have a little fun with your husband.

Ask your dry cleaners if they specialize in cleaning and preserving wedding dresses. They may do a bang-up job on suits, but that is different from cleaning a wedding dress. You can also ask the shop where you bought your dress for their suggestions. If you don't have luck there, look online or in the good old Yellow Pages. You can purchase gown-cleaning and preservation kits in stores and online for approximately $100 and up.

You can then take or mail your gown to the place that you've selected. Many dry cleaners have a drive-thru so you don't even have to get out of the car; and many specialists offer pick up and delivery — how easy is that?

Finally, once it's finished, follow the cleaner's storage instructions. Many often advise keeping it stored in a closet or under the bed, not in an attic or basement where temperatures and climates can vary and damage your dress.

Pretty simple, right? So often we make a mountain out of a molehill if given the opportunity. Don't do that at the expense of your wedding dress. You'll regret it in a few years when it looks dull, dingy and faded.

After the Wedding: Do's and Don'ts

DO FREEZE THE TOP TIER OF YOUR WEDDING CAKE. It really doesn't taste that bad the following year, and besides, it's tradition for you and your hubby to eat it on your first anniversary.

DON'T JUST THROW IT IN THE FREEZER. Call the bakery that made your cake and ask them about the best way to freeze it.

DO WHAT YOU FEEL COMFORTABLE WITH WHEN DECIDING WHETHER TO CHANGE YOUR NAME. It's the new millennium. Change your name, hyphenate it, or make up a new one. These days, anything goes; just make sure you do what you and your husband want to do.

DO MAKE SURE YOU HAVE AN OFFICIAL CERTIFIED COPY OF YOUR MARRIAGE CERTIFICATE BEFORE YOU CHANGE ANYTHING. This is the paper with the seal on it that you receive in the mail about two to four weeks after the wedding, not the license you buy before.

DO ORDER TWO COPIES OF YOUR MARRIAGE CERTIFICATE. Most places, like the Department of Motor Vehicles and the Social Security Office, need to see an original, no photocopies, so it's best to have more than one, just in case.

DO MAKE SURE YOU CHANGE YOUR NAME WITH THE SOCIAL SECURITY OFFICE FIRST. You are who your

Social Security number says you are. Everything is linked through that, so take care of them first!

Don't forget to change... your driver's license, car note, insurance, paycheck, passport, credit cards, house bills, banking information, frequent flyer miles, magazine subscriptions, and anything else with your name on it!

Do get a written appraisal for your ring. Your jeweler should provide your husband with written details about the ring's clarity, carats, etc., that your husband can use for insurance purposes.

Do insure your diamond ring. Hopefully it's too expensive not to do this.

Do be respectful and don't ask your husband how much the ring cost. He'll share the details with you if he wants to do so. Otherwise, don't ask no matter how much it kills you!

Do get the ring cleaned regularly. Most jewelry stores will clean it for you, while you wait, for free. Diamonds really sparkle when they're clean!

Do check the setting annually. Take it to a jeweler and make sure that your precious stone(s) is still set securely. Sometimes they get knocked loose and you wouldn't want to lose them!

Don't ever leave your diamond(s) with a jeweler you don't know. It's too easy for them to swap out the diamonds if they practice shady business. If you must leave your diamond, be careful. Ask friends and family to refer a reputable jeweler.

DON'T ASK FOR DETAILS ABOUT HIS BACHELOR PARTY. And don't give up too many about your bachelorette party either. Hopefully you trust each other, so you really don't need to know.

DO DOCUMENT THIS SPECIAL TIME. Keep a journal, or write details about your new life on notecards and put them in a pretty photo album. Do something to remember these precious moments as a newlywed.

Wives' Words

WHAT DID YOU EXPECT THE FIRST YEAR OF MARRIAGE TO BE LIKE?

"I thought the first year was supposed to be the 'honeymoon' phase where everything was lovey-dovey. The honeymoon phase ended after the honeymoon!"

—NANCY, MARRIED TWO YEARS

"I thought the first year would be no different than living together. NOT TRUE. Marriage is a living institution and you have no idea what to expect until you are in it."

—RACHEL, MARRIED 12 YEARS

"I expected it to be good and bad because each relationship goes through phases. I honestly didn't expect it to be as rough as it was through the first year... I was looking for more of a 'fairy tale' type first year and that was very unrealistic."

—MONICA, MARRIED THREE YEARS

"I expected it to be blissful and a true bonding experience. It exceeded my expectations."

—ROBIN, MARRIED SIX YEARS

"I thought we would have a lot more fun than we actually did. It was work from the start."   —HOPE, MARRIED 14 YEARS

"I did not imagine anything and it was more than anything I could have ever imagined."

—WANDA, MARRIED NINE YEARS

"I expected my marriage to be very easy. My husband and I dated for five years prior to getting married and lived together most of that time, so I thought being married was going to be a breeze. Whoever said that if you live with a person, when you marry them things would be the same... not so."

—QUISA, MARRIED ONE YEAR

"I thought we would instantly have this solid partnership/ marriage because we communicated very well. We eventually built a solid partnership/marriage, but it took much work and continues to take more work than I ever thought it would."

—NDIDI, MARRIED SIX YEARS

2

For Better or For Worse

TACKLING CHANGE, FEAR, AND THE NEWLYWED JITTERS

Once you happily say those two huge words, "*I do*," your relationship with your man will be forever changed. Let me say that one more time. Once you happily say those two big words, "*I do*," your relationship with your man will be forever changed.

How could a ceremony, a fabulous party, and a piece of paper change everything? The relationship you had before marriage was like already being married without it being official, right? Wrong! It was and is different. Why don't people warn you about this? I have absolutely no clue. They're probably too busy telling you how happy you are, and how happy you will be once you're married. Happiness is great, but what about the other emotions that you may feel at some point during this huge transition, like fear, anxiety, frustration, nervousness — did I mention fear? I wish someone would have waved a big red warning flag in front of my face so that I could have been more prepared.

So many brides dreamed of getting married their whole lives. Happy, perfect, fairytale dreams. Not stressful, imperfect, realistic dreams. Little did we realize how scary getting married can be. Change is frightening — and normal, and there are a ton of changes that come with getting married. These changes and all of the emotions that accompany them cause what I call the newlywed jitters. Catching a case of the newlywed jitters means that you may feel nervous, a little uncomfortable, or even scared as hell of your new union and all that comes with it. But there is hope! When you expect and accept change, you can proactively try and make things better instead of worse. If you understand that your relationship is entering a period of change and growth, then you will think more clearly and make wiser decisions to lead your marriage up a positive road. Consider this chapter to be your big red flag.

There are many things you should and shouldn't do to build a strong relationship. You're in it for the long haul now and it's important to help yourself and your husband catch most of the curve balls that life might throw you. Realize that you don't have all the answers and you're not expected to have them. Once the preacher declares you husband and wife, he doesn't say, "*Poof, now you know exactly how to be a happily married couple.*" It just doesn't work that way.

Don't make any more major, life-altering decisions until you are over the newlywed jitters. You have enough new things on your plate right now — a new husband, living arrangements, in-laws — so don't add anything else on top of it. Give yourselves time to learn, grow and adjust to your new life together before you stir in things like babies, moving across the country, or quitting your job to rediscover yourself.

And always fight fair. There's nothing like a big fight to stir up the newlywed jitters; and there is nothing worse than hitting below the belt with your husband and having to face him when your anger dies down. Using intimate secrets and vulnerable feelings that your man trusted you with can destroy even the strongest relationship. Once that happens, it's extremely difficult to rebuild the trust. Your husband should be the last person that you want to hurt so intimately — no matter how much he pisses you off.

Most importantly, don't forget to trust yourself. Women are blessed with instincts. Learn to use and trust them. Most of the time, you know deep down in your gut if something is right or wrong. That doesn't mean we always do the right thing, but most of the time we know what that right thing is.

It's OK if you don't always have all of the answers and if you make mistakes along the way. Learn from your mistakes, then use what you learn so you don't make the same mistakes again. Now is not the time to start doubting yourself. You're a strong, smart woman — act like it! Be loving, caring, understanding, compassionate, firm, giving, selfish and selfless, and stay committed to growing your relationship. Don't fear the changes that are coming your way. Make them for better, not worse!

Don't Freak Out about Becoming a Wife

The first thing that you need to do to get through the newlywed jitters is to keep your cool. Freaking out about becoming a wife is not going to fix anything. It's just going to make your head feel like you drank too many Cosmopolitans and your husband feel like he needs to drink too many Cosmopolitans.

Yes, it is intimidating, overwhelming and just freakin' scary, but you will get through it. I've dedicated a whole chapter later in the book on adjusting to your new role as a wife, but in the meantime there are a million good reasons why you shouldn't let the pressure turn you into a mad woman, and here's ten of them:

1. FREAKING OUT DOESN'T SOLVE ANYTHING. I know I said that before, but it bears repeating. Why? Because freaking out actually adds to the problem. You start with one freaked-out wife, and you will quickly gain one freaked-out husband. The biggest problem will be that he doesn't really know why either of you are freaked out. He will totally be responding to you. Once you're both freaked out, you might really need those Cosmopolitans.

2. YOU'RE IN CONTROL. It might not seem like it, but you are. You get to decide what kind of wife you want to be. And even better, there are no rules. Except the ones you set for yourself — and the ones you vowed to such as no lying, cheating, disrespecting — but those are all givens anyway.

3. THERE'S NO TIME LIMIT. Stop putting so much pressure on yourself. You are married to this man for the rest of your life. You don't have to figure everything out the first day, week or month. Many veteran wives are still working on it!

4. HE DOESN'T KNOW WHAT HE'S DOING EITHER. Yeah, he may seem all cool and collected, but trust me — he's fighting off the Freak Out Demon, too. He didn't secretly receive a "how to be a husband" tool kit in the mail. You two are going through this together, so talk to each other. You're partners, remember?

5. YOU DON'T HAVE TO BE PERFECT. Since it's impossible to be perfect, I suggest that you stop trying. There are no right and wrongs here. You will do a whole lot of things the way you'd like them to be done and a whole lot of things that make you wish you could rewind time and do it again. Congratulations, you're human.

6. HE LOVES YOU. You're stressed and worried because you want to make him happy. You want to be the best wife. Hello! He loves you. He married you. You already make him happy and guess what? You are the best wife he has. It doesn't matter that you are the only one. You're still his best.

7. IT'S WHAT YOU WANT. You chose to get married and become a wife. You got what you wanted; don't freak out about it now! Remember back to the warm and fuzzy feelings you used to get just thinking about being "Mrs. So & So."

8. BEING A WIFE IS A BEAUTIFUL THING. It really is. Try really hard to relax, to put the pressure and fear out of your mind. Take a moment to realize how blessed you are. You found him. The Love of Your Life. And he loves you, too. He put the ring on your finger and made the

commitment. If you freak out, you miss out on that wonderful feeling.

9. YOU CAN HANDLE IT! It's really not that hard — at least not all of the time. You know more than you think you know, so don't over-think yourself into a tizzy. Relax and go with the flow. Remember that you are a confident, intelligent woman. There are times when you will have to step up to some challenges, and there are times when you can just chill out on cruise control. Either way, you can handle it.

10. YOU ARE NOT ALONE. Most people freak out when they are mad, sad, scared, afraid and feel like they are the only person in the world that does not have a clue about what the hell is going on. You are not that "only person." There are approximately two million other new wives that will get married this year and have absolutely no clue either. Don't freak out about it; instead, reach out for a little support.

Do Utilize The Four C's of Marriage

Always remember and rely on what I call the Four C's (cornerstones) of Marriage — *communication, creativity, compromise and commitment.* It wasn't too long ago that you were agonizing over the Four C's of diamonds — cut, clarity, carat and color. Just like the four things that helped to mold your diamond, these are the four things that can help to shape your relationship; and help chill the newlywed jitters. At least one, if not all of the Four C's can be very helpful in even the toughest situations. Use them constantly and they will help to make the bumpy transition into married life a little bit smoother. They are by far the most essential tools you need to make your marriage thrive. If you incorporate these into the foundation of your relationship, you can rest assured that you are building a strong, flexible base that should withstand the many quakes that may come your way.

It's safe to say that virtually every Do and Don't in this book is tied in some way to one of the Four C's. That being said, they deserve to be broken down — so that your marriage never will be.

Communication (THE FIRST C) IS THE ACT OF CONVEYING INFORMATION THROUGH WORDS OR EXPRESSIONS.

Wifey's translation — *"the act of figuring out how to tell your husband what you really don't know how to say or what you meant to say in the first place; and/or figuring out what he wants or is trying to tell you, too."*

Communication is key to a successful marriage. You've probably heard this quote time and time again. So many times, in fact, that I have no idea who said it first. Well, guess what ladies? As over-used as this line is, it's absolutely true. You've got to know how to communicate with your husband. Be it through words, gestures or signals. It is extremely important that you both figure out a way to clearly (yes, I said clearly) express your needs, wants and feelings.

It's nearly impossible to have a happy, thriving relationship without being able to effectively communicate with your spouse. As necessary as it is, though, it's not always that simple. Some couples master communication quickly while others go through several battles before understanding the best way it will work for them.

I am a firm believer in talking. That you should be able to verbally communicate (or learn how to) with the person you married. There should be no human being closer to you than your spouse; therefore, being able to speak about your needs, wants and feelings (especially for a woman) is critical. As I said earlier, it's easy for me to tell you to do this, but figuring out *how* to do it is the challenge. And it's something that you and your spouse will have to learn together.

Please don't misconstrue this advice as a pass to talk, talk, talk your husband to death. While I believe that you need to *know how* to verbally communicate with your husband, you also need to know when to shut up. There may be other more effective ways to convey your wants, thoughts or needs than speaking or screaming them at him. This is something that only you can learn — through trial and error. Knowing when to bite your tongue and when to let it loose is a skillful art that every wife must learn to master.

In the meantime, there are many factors to consider that play into verbally communicating effectively with your man. Is he a talker, or does he suddenly have to make a phone call whenever a serious topic comes up? Does he have a strong self-esteem, or feel attacked every time you bring up an issue? Do you wait to tell him something is wrong until you are at your breaking point and furious; or do you have to have a serious talk every five minutes if things are not going your way? The list can go on… and on… and on.

It can take some time to figure it all out, but it is worth *every* minute you spend to make sure that you two are moving forward together and that you're on the same page. When they say that marriage takes work, this is one of those areas that needs continuous work. Don't skimp on this or you'll regret it. Here are some suggestions to start you off.

- TRY THE STRAIGHT-FORWARD APPROACH. Let him know that you would like to have a conversation about how you two can communicate effectively. Ask him what works for him; and share with him what works for you.

- DON'T ATTACK HIM OR PUT HIM ON THE DEFENSIVE. If he feels like you're coming at him like he's doing something wrong, he'll shut down. Use words like *"I feel"* and *"we both need to"* not *"you do this"* or *"you always."*

- PAY ATTENTION TO SOME OF THE NON-VERBAL COMMUNICATION — SIGNS AND GESTURES — THAT HE SENDS. Some of this knowledge will come from trial and error. If you approach him with the words *"We need to talk"* and he stiffens up, grabs a beer, and hesitantly says, *"About what?"* you need to realize that might not be the best way to start a conversation.

- DON'T GET TOO EMOTIONAL. The raving-lunatic-bitch and the crying-hysterically-oversensitive-little-girl routines are both turnoffs and non-productive. Take a deep breath and a big-girl pill, and have a calm, straight-forward conversation.

- THINK ABOUT HIS VIEW. Whenever you are communicating with anyone, especially your husband, be considerate and think about him — his thoughts, feelings and needs.

Commitment (THE SECOND C) IS PROMISING, OBLIGATING OR DEDICATING YOURSELF TO SOMEONE OR SOMETHING.

Wifey's translation — *"a promise by him to love, cherish, honor, think I'm fabulous, and stay with me whether I am*

PMS-ing, burn dinner every night, grow a mole on my neck like his great aunt, or if my perfectly perky C cup drops down to my navel after breastfeeding three of our future children."

Now that's the kind of commitment that I'm talking about. This is where the whole ball and chain thing comes into play. You are committed to each other — fitted together with indestructible steel. For better or for worse. Curlers in your hair and all.

Just remember, ladies, it goes both ways. Just as you expect him to stay committed to you through all of your ups and downs, you need to accept him and his expanding beer-belly, too.

I joke cautiously about these things, because there is an element of seriousness to what seems superficial. You and your husband made a lifelong commitment to each other and your marriage. There will be many things — events, situations, people — that will test that commitment.

It might be something that seems as shallow as him losing all of his hair before he turns 30. When you met and married him, he had a gorgeous and full head of hair. You made a commitment to the man with lots of locks, not some balding guy who suddenly looks more like his father than himself, right? Wrong. You made it to both. For better or worse. With or without hair.

Everyday events can really test your commitment. Built up over time, the fact that he never helps you with the dishes, believe it or not, can make you ask, *"When I said, 'I do,' did I make a commitment to doing the dishes for the rest of our lives, too?"*

Or it might be something more serious, like the loss of employment, a crippling car accident and, dare I say it, the temptation to be unfaithful.

When you make a commitment, especially to marriage, you are supposed to do whatever is necessary to support and keep that commitment flourishing. There will be times when you look back on your fabulous wedding day and think, "*I didn't commit to this!*" But you did. With very few exceptions — for instance, I'm not suggesting that you stay committed to a man who secretly has five other wives — you need to keep your commitment close to your heart and remind yourself of that promise when life happens and challenges start to come your way. It's easy to stay committed when things are going smoothly, but it is when obstacles arise that you need to rely on your commitment to center both of you and carry you through.

If you ever feel overwhelmed, confused or unsure of your pledge to the marriage, don't worry. It's OK to have fears, doubts and quite frankly to think, "*Hey, this is not what I thought I signed up for.*" What's not OK is to keep this train of thought. Instead of letting those feelings become dominant in your marriage, let them be signals that you need to reaffirm your commitment. OK, let's stop right here. I don't mean renew your vows with more flowers, champagne or guests. You don't even need your husband for this.

You can review your vows. Set aside some quiet time to recite them to yourself. So many people are so in awe the day they get married that they have no clue what their vows are — the words they actually repeated and pledged to uphold. If you don't have a printed copy, look at your wedding video and write down the words that were given to you. Know what you promised.

Or if you wrote your vows yourself, take out that folded up piece of paper you clutched in your sweaty palm on your wedding day and read it. Remember that day. Remember that feeling. Remember why you agreed to marry your husband. Allow it to calm you. Hopefully this will also bring clarity and reaffirm your commitment.

If you or your husband are not committed to making your marriage work, chances are it won't. So don't just make a commitment on your wedding day and leave it in a treasure box with the other mementos. Use it. Call on it. Remind yourself that it exists. You need that unwavering pledge to each other. You need to use it. It should be the ground you stand on every day that supports you and your husband.

Compromise (THE THIRD C) IS WHEN EACH SIDE AGREES TO CONCEDE IN SOME WAY TO REACH A WORKABLE SOLUTION.

Wifey's translation — *"sometimes you have to give up a little to get a little and try things his way even if you know that your opinion is the best, most effective and undeniably right!"*

You cannot have a successful marriage without two people who are willing to compromise. It's impossible! Know that you *have to* compromise with your husband to make your marriage work. Yes, those are strong words — *"have to"* — but you do.

Compromising is a big part of going from "me" to "we," and I am willing to bet my wedding china that you have already been faced with several compromising situations, especially if you had a traditional wedding. You wanted a band, he wanted his co-worker to deejay; you wanted vanilla poundcake, he wanted chocolate — any of this ringing a bell?

I'll assume you two came out of this without any major war wounds — you did make it down the aisle, right? It sounds silly to go to battle over cake but, believe me stranger, more miniscule things have caused huge rifts in many relationships. When you have two people who believe they are entitled to have everything their way, who are stubborn and hold out just to prove a point, it doesn't matter if you are disagreeing about how may children you want to bring into the world, what color to paint the dining room, or who should be the next American Idol. That selfish kind of behavior will shoot down your marriage before you even know what hit you.

Compromising will transform many of those tirades into productive discussions and bring a peaceful resolution more quickly. I have a few simple rules that can help regulate the process.

Rule 1 – BOTH OF YOU HAVE TO COMPROMISE.

It shouldn't always be *you* giving in and it shouldn't always be your husband either. If one of you always gets your way and the other always doesn't, that's not a marriage — it's a dictatorship. Last time I checked, most people don't like dictators too much. Resentment tends to build, which can lead to suppressed anger, unhappiness and mutiny. Make sure you *both* do the compromising.

Rule 2 – PICK YOUR BATTLES WISELY.

I'm certain that you've heard this before, but you would be surprised by how many people get down and dirty over something they really don't even care about. If you just cannot bear to spend Christmas morning at his parents' house in Miami because there's no snow and you'll miss your mom's famous macaroni and cheese, by all means tell him this is a big one for you. But if you can get over spending a week on South Beach in the depth of the winter (mojitos anyone?) and can convince your mother to make you some mac and cheese when you get back, pack your presents and your bathing suit — you've just picked your battle wisely.

Rule 3 – WHEN YOU GIVE IN MORE THAN HIM, DON'T THROW IT IN HIS FACE.

It belittles the nice thing that you just did; and it's just not cool. Also, don't keep score. If you both are compromising for the sake of your relationship and out of love for each other, it will inevitably balance out. He might bend more on something twice in a row, because they were things that worked out better that way and that's all right.

Rule 4 – IF YOU ARE DEADLOCKED, AGREE TO DISAGREE AND COME BACK TO IT LATER.

Later may be in an hour, some time that evening, or in two weeks. But if you're really stuck, don't force it. Take some time, agree to disagree and, most importantly, agree to think of ways to come to a peaceful resolution. Compromise is not one person giving up something for the other. Most of the time, both of you will need to work together and each give up a little for you both to be satisfied.

Creativity (THE FOURTH C) IS THE ABILITY TO BE ORIGINAL AND USE YOUR IMAGINATION.

Wifey's translation — *"the ability to use what you've got (and some of what you don't) to keep your relationship hot and to get what you want without him realizing that's exactly what you're doing."*

It sounds a little deceptive, and I would never suggest such a thing. Yeah right. Seriously though, I'm not telling you to use your creative genius in a negative or manipulative way. I am just suggesting that creativity can be useful in all areas of your marriage and many times taking a second to think about things — outside of the box — could work to your advantage... I mean mutually benefit your marriage.

For instance, you may find the need to creatively think of a way to get your husband to start helping you do the dishes. Coincidentally, you are in the mood for sex every night that he happens to help you. Believe me, he'll start to put two and two together and become an expert dishwasher in no time. Both of you are clearly benefiting here. Sex and dishes are both getting done, and on the same night. Who could ask for more?

Creativity not only makes things happen, it can make them more interesting. One of the most common fears that people have about marriage is that it becomes "old and boring." Creativity is "old and boring's" kryptonite. It keeps your marriage fresh, original and exciting. Creativity can break a monotonous routine and put some spunk back into your lives.

Yes, it's the obvious; sex and creativity are an explosive combination — literally. The things that creativity and variety can do for your sex life are way too lengthy — and risqué — to include in this book. Just let it be known that mixing sex and creativity is highly encouraged.

But please know that creativity can be just as powerful in other areas, too. It adds depth to your relationship. When you take the time to get creative, to plan something special, to take your husband's thoughts and feelings into consideration, it can strengthen your bond. Instead of taking him to his usual favorite restaurant or bar for his birthday, try some place new that you know he would like and has never experienced. Think about what would really make him happy — maybe it's a hotdog with sauerkraut dinner, watching the Atlanta Braves at Turner Field, or maybe it's not dinner at all. Maybe *you* are dinner with some of his favorite sweets all over your body. Oops, my creativity took me right back to sex.

When you think creatively, the possibilities are endless. There is no reason why you can't or shouldn't be creative in all areas of your relationship — problem-solving, lovemaking, holiday planning, money-making, house-cleaning, the list could go on and on.

If your marriage starts to feel stale or "old and boring" at any time, know that you have the power to change that by thinking creatively. If you get stuck and don't know what to do, or just don't have a creative bone in your body (everybody has, you just haven't discovered it yet) ask people who you trust for ideas. Or if you don't want people in your business, read a book. There are self-help books for everything you could possibly think of these days including *How to Do Just About Everything*. Really, I saw it online. Or search the Web for ideas. Between websites, chat rooms and blogs, there are more than enough resources to help you get creative.

To keep your marriage thriving, you have to actively make this happen. Who knows, maybe your initiative might spark some in your husband. Things really get interesting once both of you are thinking outside of the box. Creativity is not only one of the four cornerstones in your marriage, it's perhaps the most enjoyable one to use.

Don't Include the "D-Word" in Your Vocabulary

You should never, yes I said *never*, threaten your husband with the "D-word" — divorce. There are just some things that should never be said, especially if you are not prepared to start receiving or paying alimony checks. There are just some lines that should never be crossed and throwing divorce in your husband's face is one of them. I don't know any other way to say it than it's just bad. Bad fighting, bad taste and definitely bad karma.

In fact, erase it out of your mind. If you want to have a thriving marriage, divorce should never come up. It's an out. A safety hatch. A way to not give one hundred percent. And a way to end what you are working so hard to keep.

I know I sound a little hardcore here, but there is some logic to this train of thought. Have you ever heard of the expression *"failure is not an option"*? Well, you should adopt the mindset that divorce is not an option, either. If you know and rely on the fact that you can always run down to the courthouse and undo *"'til death do us part"* before you're dead, it takes the finality out of it.

You married your husband because you believe in the sacrament and institution of marriage. You believe that your love and dedication to each other will protect you through the hard times. Trust in your beliefs and take your hand off of the emergency exit door. It may be there, but there are times when you just shouldn't use it. When you are on airplane cruising at an altitude of 30,000 feet and turbulence starts bouncing the plane around, you might get a little scared. Things that are unknown and uncontrollable can be frightening. You try to be calm but decide you've had enough and want out. If you open that emergency exit door, you are taking down the plane and everyone in it.

You didn't need it when you were sitting there peacefully on the runway, but thousands of miles aboveground when it got a little rocky you were ready to pull the hatch. Don't. That is definitely not the time to do it. It's the easy and often most damaging way out. Making life-altering decisions during emotional and difficult times should always be avoided. Come out of the storm before you start looking for lawyers. If you ever reach a point in your marriage where things are that turbulent, seek help before you open that door. A therapist, doctor, religious leader — some professional who can help to get your marriage back on track.

Yes, in this generation, divorce not only exists, it happens to nearly 50 percent of marriages. So are there ever times that divorce is warranted? Of course there is. But if you start your marriage with the positive mindset of making it work — emergency exits not included — you have a much better chance of reaching that 50 year — not the 50 percent mark.

⊗

For Better or For Worse: Do's and Don'ts

DO KNOW THAT YOUR RELATIONSHIP IS DIFFERENT NOW. As I've said previously, don't panic. Different doesn't mean bad, it just means not the same. You are legally and emotionally tied to someone now, in some way, shape or form that changes your relationship.

DO KEEP LEARNING ABOUT EACH OTHER. It's impossible to know everything about somebody, especially since people change. Keep trying to learn more.

DO ENCOURAGE EACH OTHER TO FOLLOW YOUR DREAMS. Talk about them, encourage them, and live them.

DO BE HIS BIGGEST CHEERLEADER WHEN HE ACCOMPLISHES HIS DREAMS. Sing his praises to the world and make sure he knows you're proud.

DO SET GOALS. Personal goals, family goals, short-term goals, and long-term goals. Have something to strive for together, and individually.

DO TALK TO YOUR HUSBAND. And if you can't get it out in words, get it out on paper. Encourage him to do the same.

DO CONSIDER HIS FEELINGS. They may act tough and hard on the outside, but, yes, men have feelings, too. It's your job to see through the machismo and to consider his feelings, too.

DON'T THINK THAT LONG-MARRIED GUARANTEES STRONG-MARRIED. There are millions of couples that stay married and unhappy. It's not just about quantity, but quality, too.

DON'T FIGHT IN PUBLIC. Never air your dirty laundry in public. Bite your tongue if you have to, and keep arguments behind close doors where they belong.

DON'T FIGHT IN PUBLIC. That's worth repeating twice.

DON'T EXPECT TO LIKE EVERYTHING HE DOES. It's impossible. Enjoy the good and accept the bad.

DON'T BE OVERLY JEALOUS. If your husband is chatting with a pretty, size 6 cutie at a party, don't freak out — even if he's drooling. You don't want to look insane and ridiculous. Having casual conversations with beautiful people is still allowed once you're married.

DON'T ASK DUMB QUESTIONS. Think about things before they fly out of your mouth. Have faith in your husband and your marriage. Don't assume, unless he gives you good reason, that he's doing something wrong. Ask smart and fair questions. You're entitled to basic information, but you are not a legal prosecutor.

DON'T ASK A QUESTION IF YOU DON'T WANT THE AN-SWER. What was his nickname for his ex-girlfriend? Are you better in bed than she was? Do you really want to know? And really, what difference does it make?

DON'T TRY AND CHANGE EACH OTHER. You married your spouse for who he is (or you should have), not for who you want him to be.

DO ACCEPT YOUR SPOUSE FOR WHO HE IS. If you don't, you probably shouldn't have married him.

DO KEEP DATING. Each other.

DON'T DISCUSS HOUSEHOLD BUSINESS ON A DATE. It kills the mood.

DON'T LET RESENTMENT BUILD UP. It's like a little kid blowing a really big bubble… eventually it's going to pop and make everything really sticky.

DON'T ASSUME. You know, the whole ass out of you and me thing.

DO HAVE A POSITIVE ATTITUDE. Why should the cup be half-empty when it is half-full?

DON'T PLACE BLAME WHEN FIGHTING. Even if it's his fault. Say, "*I feel,*" instead of "*you did.*" It will get you much farther.

DON'T FIGHT FOR CONTROL. Neither one of you should control the other. Marriage is a partnership, not a dictatorship.

Wives' Words

WHAT WAS YOUR BIGGEST FEAR ABOUT GETTING MARRIED?

"Losing my unique individuality."

—TOMIKA, MARRIED THREE YEARS

"Getting a divorce. My parents are divorced and so are my husband's parents, so I was always worried that I didn't have a firsthand example of what it takes to make a marriage work."

—NANCY, MARRIED TWO YEARS

"I was afraid that married life would change me into the 'ball and chain.'"

—CHERYL, MARRIED FIVE YEARS

"Not being able to cut the mustard as a wife because I grew up in a single-parent household and didn't have a model to follow firsthand."

—MONICA, MARRIED THREE YEARS

"We had been together for four years and already had a child together, but I was still worried about 'the change' from lovable happy adorable newlywed to 'the ball and chain.' I did also fear making the wrong decision."

—ALLISON, MARRIED 12 YEARS

"Boredom."

—RHONDA, MARRIED 20 YEARS

"I've been waiting in a quiet fear, as if I'm watching a scary movie, for the change that everyone has advised me is around the corner."

—JENNIFER, MARRIED FOUR MONTHS

"Losing my sense of independence/freedom."

—HOPE, MARRIED 14 YEARS

"Occasionally, I would lose my mind and the fear of getting divorced would grip my heart, but my husband and I took our vows seriously and adopted 'divorce is not an option' as one of our mantras."

—ANGELA, MARRIED 16 YEARS

"Giving up my freedom... Being able to come and go as I pleased, not worrying about anyone except for me! Well, all that changed..."

—QUISA, MARRIED ONE YEAR

"Suffocating — having no personal space."

—NDIDI, MARRIED SIX YEARS

☙

WHAT DO YOU WISH SOMEONE WOULD HAVE WARNED YOU ABOUT BEING MARRIED?

"Don't assume that your friends will remain your 'friends' after matrimony. No one will respect your marriage more than you and if you share too much with these 'friends' some may use it against you."

—CHERYL, MARRIED FIVE YEARS

"A friend's mom once told us that you don't want to be with your best friend twenty-four hours a day, so what makes you think you'd want to be with your spouse twenty-four hours a day? It is natural for both of you to want some space."

—ROBIN, MARRIED SIX YEARS

"That sometimes it gets dull."

—WANDA, MARRIED NINE YEARS

"That there are good days and BAD days. There are good weeks and BAD weeks. But most importantly... to be able to say we have been married fifty years takes going through some trials to get there."

—RACHEL, MARRIED 12 YEARS

"I guess to sum it up — marriage is hard work. To have a really good marriage that lasts, you have to be willing to work at it even when you don't feel like it."

—ALLISON, MARRIED 12 YEARS

"I wish someone would have warned me about the pressure you feel to keep up appearances when you first get married. We argue at times and initially it was scary to argue or let anyone see us argue because I thought they would look at us like 'they ain't gonna make it.'"

—JENNIFER, MARRIED FOUR MONTHS

"That it really takes a strong commitment to work on the marriage. It's not the fairy tale you see on TV; it can be rough."

—HOPE, MARRIED 14 YEARS

"I wish someone would have told me to forgive a little quicker, not take myself so doggone seriously, and don't waste one hot minute trying to change my husband!"

—ANGELA, MARRIED 16 YEARS

"I wish someone would have warned me about living with your beau before getting married. It's just not a good idea. Going into the marriage with a fresh, clean slate; both parties willing to adjust to each other is key."

—QUISA, MARRIED ONE YEAR

"The constant work and compromise needed to build and maintain a solid marriage."

—NDIDI, MARRIED SIX YEARS

3

Mrs. Who?

GRADUATING FROM GIRLFRIEND TO WIFE, GRACEFULLY

Mrs. Who? Me? A wife? That sounds so official — official and old. When I think of a "wife," I think of my mother, her friends, and my aunties — not me! I can still remember so clearly the first time somebody called me "*Mrs. Robertson.*" I was reading a magazine in the waiting room at the doctor's office and almost missed my appointment. It took the nurse saying my new name three times, plus a tap on my shoulder, for me to realize that she was referring to me.

What does a wife do, anyway? And how is she supposed to act? Does my husband expect me to change from the person I've been? Do I have to cook him dinner every night now that I'm his wife? Does he expect me to keep the house spotless, too? Is that how a wife acts? I've never been a wife before, how am I supposed to know what to do?

OK, slow down, stop right there, and don't panic — like I did when I got married. The truth is, there is no one way that a wife has to act. You should honor your wedding vows by being loving, faithful and respectful, but other than that it is entirely up to you. You and your husband (but mostly you) get to decide what other wifely duties you choose to do, or not do. *You* get to define your role as a wife, not society, old stereotypes, television shows and, no, not even your mother.

Here's another big red warning flag that I wish somebody would have waved for me, *do not attempt to be Superwifey!* Who is Superwifey? She's a compulsive, obsessive woman who does everything herself. She cooks, cleans, irons, shops, works full-time, exercises more than five times a week, and probably changes the oil in the car — you name it, she does it. Superwifey is perfect, and she's impossible to be. Let me save you the time and trouble — don't even try!

I tried and it was the most horrifying week of my life. OK, it lasted a little bit longer than that, but it was truly horrifying. The pressure of trying to make sure that I was doing everything mentioned above, and then some, while staying sane was exhausting. I wasn't the most pleasant person to be around either. I was breaking my back to make sure that everything in our lives was "perfect" (because I was Superwifey) and getting resentful when I thought that Napoleon didn't appreciate it. It wasn't that he didn't appreciate it, it was just not necessary. It really didn't matter to either one of us, especially to him, if the bathroom floor was so clean that you could eat off of it. And he was fine with dropping off the dry-cleaning on his way to work, since he drove by it everyday.

It's probably not your husband who puts the most pressure on you to become Superwifey — it's you! So many of us "new millennium" women want to take care of everything ourselves, and prove that we can handle just as much, if not more, than a man. Well, you're married now and fortunately you don't have to do everything yourself. You have a husband, a partner, and that's one of the best things about being married. There's someone there to share things with and, dare I say it, to *help* you. That's a really great thing. Be happy about it, and don't stress yourself out by trying to do everything yourself.

As I said before, being a wife is different from being someone's girlfriend. You've committed your life to someone and you should receive more respect for that. Accept and cherish it. It's a wonderful thing. Meanwhile, don't let the title of "wife" intimidate you. Be the type of wife that *you* want to be. If you both work and make money, keep on doing it. If you mow the lawn and he cooks dinner and that's the way the two of you like it, don't change. This is not the sixties and you are not June and Ward Cleaver from *Leave it to Beaver*. *You* have to define your own roles for your marriage; no one else can do it for you. So relax, take your time, and most of it will come naturally.

Don't Translate Gaining a Husband into Losing Your Identity

Just because you're married now, doesn't mean you're not you. You are who you are and no ring, title, new last name, or man is going to change that. Your circumstances changed, you didn't. You are still the same woman you were before you added wife to the list of titles you already have.

"Added" is the key word here. You added a husband to your life. That doesn't mean that you have to take anything away. You are still a woman, a daughter, a sister, a friend, a co-worker, a tennis player, a movie lover, a chocoholic, or whatever your passions may be — all of this should not disappear at the sound of "*I do.*" Aren't those things the reason he fell in love with you anyway? Because *you* are the only *you* in the world? If you let go of your identity, you'll not only lose yourself, but more than likely your marriage, too. You came first. You can't have a happy marriage without you being a real part of it.

Don't Let Anyone Convince You to Give Up Your Career

The life of the working woman has improved tremendously compared to our mothers' generation. Remember the perfume commercial, "*I can bring home the bacon, fry it up in a pan, and never let him forget he's a man*"? Well, today, not only do we bring home the bacon and fry it up, we buy it, sell it, market it, distribute it, advertise it, manage it, and probably own the whole damn company!

Today women are smashing through the glass ceiling at record-breaking speed. Gone are the days of having to stay at home, iron your husband's shirts all day, and have a steak and potatoes dinner waiting for him when he walks through the door. The women of the new millennium have choices.

We can choose to work, we can choose to stay home, and we can choose from a wide variety of housekeeping and food takeout services to help keep us sane.

While all of these choices are good, they can add a lot of stress and pressure on career-thriving women. It can be very challenging trying to balance a demanding career while you are establishing the most important relationship of your life. But while it's not always easy, it can be done. Fortunately it doesn't have to be an either/or choice between career and marriage. Here are four tips to help you break the glass ceiling without breaking your marriage.

- REALIZE THAT YOU HAVE CHOICES. You do not have to walk away from your five- or six-figure salary, the corner office with windows, the health & spa benefits, and the numerous other perks you earned along the way unless *you* want to do so. You can still maintain your career while you build a partnership with your husband.

- MAKE TIME FOR YOUR MARRIAGE. If you're on the career track, long working hours might be an obstacle to an optimal marriage. You have to make time outside of work for your husband. If you choose to do both, then you have to do both. You can't just work and ignore your marriage, just like you can't commit to a job and not show up.

- TALK TO YOUR HUSBAND. Make sure he knows how important your career is to you. I assume part of the reason he loves you is for your drive, determination and all of the other superb qualities that landed you the great position you hold now. I hope that you two talked about this before you got married; if not, now is the time to share your feelings.

- SET BOUNDARIES. At work and at home. For instance, you don't work on his birthday, or past 9 p.m. Or you only bring work home under extreme circumstances and it never comes into the bedroom. You have to set boundaries that work for you, your husband and your job, but you don't have to announce them to the world. Your boss, co-workers or your husband might not understand or like the boundaries that you've set. Use your discretion about who needs to know what. The most important thing is that *you* have them and use them.

Don't Worry, You Don't Have to Turn Into Your Mother

Yikes! Isn't that every woman's fear? As much as you love your mother, the last thing that you want to do is be her. Just because you are someone's wife doesn't mean that you automatically become your mother.

Chances are, your mother is how you identify with being a wife. You watched her do it. Some of our mothers stayed married, and some of them became single mothers. Either way, you do not have to follow the same path that your mother did. You have the power and the freedom to choose your own way.

Yes, there are some things that are just plain unavoidable. The first time you hear yourself saying the same phrase your mother said every day of your childhood — the same phrase that you swore a million times you never would say — you might quickly slip into a panic attack. Stop and breathe. It's life. It happens to all of us; and it's not necessarily a bad thing.

When it comes to our mothers, it is wise to adopt all of the amazingly good qualities and bypass the unspeakably bad. There are many ways that I am proud to be like my mother, and none that I am not. Come on, she is reading this book! Seriously, of course my mom has traits that I have sworn up and down I will never accept in myself. I don't have to, and neither do you. That's what makes us each special individual people.

Pay attention to what you admire about your mother (her patience, wisdom and ability to pick the perfect pair of shoes) and strive to incorporate those traits into your life. Also pay attention to the less desirable traits (her inquisitiveness, demanding-nature and ability to pick out everything that you've done wrong) and consciously block them once you see them forming. And don't feel bad about it. If you're smart enough to recognize the positive and lose the negative then she did an excellent job raising you. Besides, ask her; she's probably just as scared that she is turning into her mother, too.

Do Exercise – Regularly

Regular exercise should be an integral part of every woman's life. And no, taking Pilates once every six months or going to the gym every day for two weeks just before your Jamaican vacation doesn't count. That is not regular. That is once in a nonexistent moon. Regular is at least three times per week — every week.

Staying happy in your marriage starts with being happy with yourself. A big piece of that is your physical state. And this is not only about the way you look — I'll get to that in a minute — but most importantly about how healthy you are.

One in four women has some form of cardiovascular disease. This by far is the leading cause of death for women. It's not just your grandmother that should be concerned about this anymore. Because of our lack of exercise and the atrocious way we eat, heart disease is affecting younger age groups, too. Do you really want to risk your health at such a wonderful time in your life? You just said, "*'Til death do us part.*" Don't rush it.

OK, now to the way we look. Not only does exercising regularly help reduce the risk of several life-threatening diseases, it also helps you stay "fine." Feeling good about the way you look is important. It helps you maintain your swagger, your sense of style, and your sex appeal. It also builds confidence and a better sex life.

It may sound sexist, but it's true. Ask any newlywed man what he fears the most about getting married, and I guarantee you that "*my wife will let herself go*" will be one of his top three answers. Most men fear that we'll gain weight, lose interest in sex, and turn into our mothers — or, even worse, their mothers. I have a very simple solution for this one — don't let it happen!

It's important that you take care of yourself, first and foremost, *for you,* and it's nice that your husband can reap the benefits, too. You can't be happy in a relationship if you're not happy with yourself. We feel better, look better, and are happier when we take care of ourselves. So do your hair, paint your toes, and make the effort to exercise. You don't have to be picture perfect every day; I wouldn't suggest that to anyone. You're not Superwifey, remember? However, make the effort to be that hot chick your husband fell in love with — more often than not.

If you were fit and exercised before you got married, you should make sure you stay fit and exercise after you get married. If you weren't, then it's time to start now. Taking care of yourself is one of the best things that you can do for your marriage. Being a healthy, confident, self-loving person will make you a better wife. There are no excuses allowed on this one. Nobody has extra time built into their day for exercise; you have to make it. It's a matter of life, death, and increasing cellulite. But before you start exercising, make sure you get your doctor's approval, then grab your Nikes and get moving.

There are countless reasons to exercise and countless ways to increase your physical activity and incorporate exercise into your daily routine. Here's a quick fifteen of each, not including the obvious "join a gym," to get you thinking…

WHY YOU SHOULD DO IT:

1. Reduces stress and depression.
2. Get to shop for a new wardrobe.
3. Low-rise jeans.
4. Boosts your sex drive.
5. Improves quality of sleep.
6. You'll feel more energetic.
7. Envious looks.

8. To get a booty like Beyoncé's and abs like Janet's.
9. Reduces your risk of heart disease and some forms of cancer (including breast).
10. Increases your confidence.
11. It feels good when you're done.
12. Because 50 is the new 35.
13. It reduces the risk of osteoporosis.
14. Did I already mention sex?
15. Your longevity depends on it.

What to do:

1. Hire a personal trainer.
2. Work out at home.
3. Take a dance class.
4. Try kickboxing.
5. Ride a bike.
6. Join a co-ed softball team with your husband.
7. Do exercise videos.
8. Walk with a friend.
9. Work out at lunchtime.
10. Walk your dog, instead of the dog walking you.
11. Have sex (yes, it burns calories!).
12. Sign up for a charity race.
13. Schedule exercise time like you schedule meetings.
14. Take the stairs.
15. Don't park in the closest parking space, every extra step counts!

Mrs. Who?: Do's and Don'ts

DO DEFINE YOUR NEW ROLES EARLY. Set the tone for your new life and your new roles as husband and wife now. Just remember, it's trial and error, so expect for things to evolve slowly over time.

DO LEARN WHEN TO LEAVE HIM ALONE. Everyone needs some space, especially a man. Don't take it personally.

DON'T EXPECT YOUR HUSBAND TO NURTURE YOU LIKE A WOMAN DOES. It's just not how most men are made. If that's what you need, call your mother, your sister or your girlfriends.

DO KNOW THAT HUSBANDS HAVE SELECTIVE HEARING. They can hear the game on television that's across the room while they're sleeping, but you can talk five feet in front of their face and they may not hear a word you're saying.

DON'T JUMP ON HIM WHEN HE WALKS THROUGH THE DOOR FROM WORK. Women are ready to vent; men need at least fifteen minutes, and a trip to the bathroom.

DON'T COMPLAIN WHEN HE WANTS TO GO OUT WITH THE BOYS. That is, as long as it's not every night of the week. Call your girls to make your plans; it's just the right excuse for a ladies night out.

DON'T NAG. Yeah right; well, just don't be so obvious about it. Don't whine or bitch about things, but do be persistent about what you need.

DON'T EVER GO THROUGH YOUR MAN'S POCKETS. Unless he is wearing them.

DON'T REPEAT YOUR HUSBAND'S SECRETS. We all need an outlet — a girlfriend, sister or mother — but if he asks you not to repeat something, don't.

DON'T TELL YOUR MOTHER EVERY INTIMATE DETAIL OF YOUR RELATIONSHIP. Or if you do, don't do it in front of your husband.

DO SLEEP IN CUTE OR SEXY PAJAMAS. Sweats and T-shirts are fine sometimes, but make the effort to slip into a satin teddy several nights a week.

DO TALK ABOUT HEALTH ISSUES. You're a team now and you need to help each other stay happy and healthy.

DON'T FEEL PRESSURED INTO DOING ALL OF THE COOKING. Many men can throw down in the kitchen — Emeril, G. Garvin, Jamie Oliver — The Naked Chef... hmmm... maybe your husband could... OK, I won't go there.

DO LEARN HOW TO COOK HIS FAVORITE MEAL. There's something special about a man and his favorite food, and a woman who can cook it for him.

Don't get mad if he doesn't like everything you cook. Ask him what he likes and doesn't like. No one should have to keep eating something they can't stand, or in this case stomach.

Do eat consciously, too. If his health dictates a restricted diet, don't chow down on a chili cheeseburger and fries while he's eating tofu. Not cool.

Don't criticize your husband's wardrobe. If you don't like something you can make suggestions, but never put him down.

Do help his sense of style... but only if he needs it. Buy him a shirt or two, but don't be offended if he doesn't like them.

Do tell him that he looks sexy in the shirt you just bought him. I bet he'll like it then.

Don't wear matching clothes. It's OK to coordinate with what your husband is wearing (both looking casual, for example), but don't take it too far. A family reunion is the only time matching shirts are acceptable — the only time!

Wives' Words

About Communication

"Lack of it can ruin the most promising relationship."
—CHERYL, MARRIED FIVE YEARS

"That's the mother of it all; it's the rock that will hold you both together!"
—WANDA, MARRIED NINE YEARS

"Men and women speak different languages. So the biggest challenge is trying not to use the female filter when deciphering what he says and does."
—NANCY, MARRIED TWO YEARS

"It's the most important thing you have. Talk until you are blue in the face and always try to understand his perspective and ask him to try to understand yours."
—RACHEL, MARRIED 12 YEARS

"Be honest, be open, and be true. Never go to bed angry with each other. I don't care if it's 3 a.m. and you can't sleep because you have something on your mind; wake up your spouse and get it off your chest."
—MONICA, MARRIED THREE YEARS

"I can't say it enough — communication is everything! Talk, talk, talk even if you think it is nothing... It could eventually be 'something,' so talk about it!"
—ALLISON, MARRIED 12 YEARS

"Communication is absolutely essential. Without it, petty concerns fester and turn into major issues."
—RHONDA, MARRIED 20 YEARS

"Be kind and respectful and offer freedom and space willingly."
—SHARON, MARRIED EIGHT YEARS

"Don't treat your marriage like you treated your courting relationship. Avoid tossing around wedding bands and divorce in an effort to convey a sense of urgency. Discussing and arguing are fine as long as your goal is to understand."
—JENNIFER, MARRIED FOUR MONTHS

"Be honest but tactful." —NDIDI, MARRIED SIX YEARS

Men don't think the way we do. What we obsess about they probably haven't even thought about. Tell them what is bothering you and talk about it and try and find a way to explain it so he gets it."
—ROBIN, MARRIED SIX YEARS

ABOUT TAKING ON THE ROLE OF WIFE

"Create your own version of what being a 'wife' means."
—NDIDI, MARRIED SIX YEARS

"Ease into it. I think a lot of women start power-tripping like 'I am the wife and what I say goes.' Treat him with respect always. Never take him for granted." —ALLISON, MARRIED 12 YEARS

"As a wife, you have lots of responsibilities, but one to be aware of is that you are still your husband's romantic partner, not just a household partner. So don't let yourself go! Make an effort to look attractive for him. Do your hair, put on a little lip-gloss. Wear that dress he likes, exercise, etc. Dress like you're single and trying to catch a man." —NANCY, MARRIED TWO YEARS

"Realize that what you have thought of as the role of the wife and what your husband thinks of as the role of the wife can be worlds away from each other." —RACHEL, MARRIED 12 YEARS

"Being someone's wife is no small task. Love your husband, support him, and always be uplifting." —MONICA, MARRIED THREE YEARS

"Run your home and your marriage like you would a successful business." —SHARON, MARRIED EIGHT YEARS

"Embracing your role as wife provides such shape and security to the marriage." —JENNIFER, MARRIED FOUR MONTHS

"Don't let anyone define that role for you. It should be decided by you and your husband, no one else. And don't be afraid to modify it as life situations change."

—CHERYL, MARRIED FIVE YEARS

4

Living Together

SHARING SPACE AND STAYING SANE

1 + 1 = 2. No matter how you add it up, there are two of you now. Talk about a big change, especially now that you've moved in together. Now you have to love each other, live together, and like it. That's a feat much easier said then done. There's someone else for you to consider now, for you to share things with, and for you to consult. I'm sure that you were not a selfish person before marriage, but there were certain things that you could get away with prior to that life-altering stroll down the aisle that you just shouldn't do now. Cooking, cleaning, decorating, playing music, watching television, having pets and entertaining company are just a few of the many things that both of you need to be considerate about once you live together.

Now that you are a part of a *we*, it doesn't mean that you are not still *you*. But you do have to add some more pronouns to your vocabulary. We, us, ours, and he are very important words for you to know and use when living with someone. It can't only be I, I, I, or me, me, me. How you adjust to becoming one part of two will set the tone of your marriage. A big part of that adjustment is living together — physically and mentally. Are you going to be defensive and selfish, or considerate and sharing?

Trust me when I say that living together is one of the biggest transitions that you go through when you get married (which is why this is one of the longest chapters in this book!). Even if you moved in together before you said your vows (no, having a toothbrush and a box of tampons at his house does not count), in some ways, living together is different when you become husband and wife.

Why is it different if you and your hubby have already been shacking up? There are hundreds of variables that might or might not change things. Maybe you have a stronger sense of commitment as husband and wife, so sharing has become easier for you. Or maybe you've been living in his apartment but it never felt like yours until you officially became his wife. Maybe you think that because you're his wife, you should cook him a hot meal every night. Or maybe now that you're both more secure in your relationship, you feel comfortable sleeping in hair curlers instead of a full face of makeup, while your husband has picked up the lovely new habit of farting in bed every night. Need I go on?

It's also different from living with a roommate. There's no intimate or emotional tie with a roommate, and you could go without seeing and speaking to your roommate for days, even weeks. So interacting and sharing yourself with each other daily can feel extremely overwhelming.

Now don't get me wrong — you don't have to and you shouldn't spend every waking moment together when you're married. As happy as you are, still floating on that newlywed high, I promise that you would get on each other's very last nerves — quickly. But you will spend more time with your spouse than anyone else, and it can be very easy to forget some of the obvious little things that you need to do daily to help make your marriage thrive.

For instance, kiss him good-bye before you leave for work. Make it a habit. Long and sexy or short and sweet, it doesn't matter as long as you do it. Also, leave him love notes around the house. E-mail or text him at work. Let him know you'd like to get to bed early tonight, but you're not very sleepy. Have fun with it. These are simple things that can make an average relationship a great one.

Talk to each other. Not just in passing, but sit down and share things with each other. Talk about your day, your family, a movie or what's going on in the world. In the same breath, I say, *don't* talk to each other. Don't make small talk when you don't need to chat. You don't have to fill every second of every day with words. It's not an awkward silence when you're happily married. It can be very relaxing to curl up on the couch with your husband and read a book or flip through a good issue of *O, The Oprah Magazine* and not break the silence for a while.

Pay attention to the needs you each have and know your spouse's habits well. It will make your days flow more smoothly. If you know he likes to do the three S's (shit, shower and shave) before breakfast, give him his space. If you've gotta have that cup of coffee before too much chit-chat in the morning, let him know that, too. Communicate your needs, read each other's signals, and most importantly respect them.

Speaking of respect, make sure that you and your husband are courteous to each other. That should be a given in all of our relationships, but so often we forget to do it. Say hello and good-bye as well as please and thank you. Thank him whether he brings you a glass of water, mows the lawn, or makes up the bed. You say thank you to the cashier at the supermarket when she gives you your change, so why wouldn't you thank the man that you married for all of the wonderful things he does?

If you haven't previously lived together, remember to talk to your husband about what is important to you. It's difficult to go from living by yourself to living with someone else — no matter how much you love him! Everyone needs their own space and privacy (even from their spouse) and especially if they're used to living alone.

You both probably have a routine; a way of doing things that might not always match up. Ironically, most couples' routines are opposites. If he's a neat freak, you can't stand to clean, or if he likes to wake up to the buzz on his alarm clock, you prefer the relaxing sounds of the radio.

Living together is about compromise. Talk to each other and figure out what you can give on and what you can't. If you get stuck on something, use your creativity. Maybe one week he gets the annoying buzzer and the next week you get the soothing music. Who knows, maybe after a month, you'll start to prefer the buzzer or he'll turn into a music lover.

Living with someone, even the love of your life, can be difficult at times. Every day will not go smoothly; however, if you incorporate these signs of affection, respect and love into your daily routine, you can look forward to enjoying them, every day, for the rest of your life together.

Whatever scenario of living together you're tackling, just remember to think about your husband, too. Both of your needs are equally important, and both of you should be happy in your new home.

Isn't it a beautiful thing when you wake up next to the man you love and realize that there are two of you now, and it's not just me, me, me?

Do Be Patient!

Patience is essential when you've just moved in together. It takes time to adjust to someone else's habits. And once you are living together permanently, you will discover many habits that you probably never noticed. After you've tipped the movers, sent the truck on its way and there is no escaping him, habits start showing themselves miraculously like food commercials as soon as you begin a new diet. They were always there, but either he was on his good behavior or you just never caught onto them.

Everyone has at least one quirky habit that a spouse probably won't discover until it's way too late to send back the wedding china. Once you're married, there's a sense of security and acceptance that allows you to let your guard down and some of your uniqueness out. For instance, you may feel like the world is ending if your spice cabinet is not arranged in alphabetical order, and he may not understand why chili powder has to go before cumin. Your husband might like to read the paper and eat his breakfast butt-naked on the sofa every morning. Maybe he kept his clothes on before you got married, because he didn't want to freak you out (which he just did). Or maybe that was fine when it was his old beat-up couch; however now that it's your new cream love seat, you might not want his bare tush blessing it every morning — no matter how cute his bottom is. Or you might find it sexy that he's naked every morning and it could lead to some really hot sex. (Just because you discover a quirky habit, don't assume that the result is going to be negative.)

Moving is stressful by itself. It takes a while to unpack the boxes, and put everything in its place. Add on the joy, fear, intimidation and host of other emotions that are flooding your body, and it could lead to some pretty heated arguments in the early days of living together after your wedding. You need to be patient with your husband and yourself. Pointing out all of his habits that have totally freaked you out will not help the situation. Besides, I'm sure he's discovering a few new things about his angel that he didn't know were hiding under your halo. Here's my top two tips for calming down and staying patient when you would like to pull a Whitney Houston and tell him, "*Hell-to-the-no!*"

1. TAKE A TIME-OUT. It's not just for kids anymore. If you know that you are about to react emotionally, if you already know that what you're about to say is going to start the fight of the century, stop! Walk away. Take a deep breath and count to 10, to 20, to 100 if you need to, in order to get yourself calm. Nothing gets solved in the heat of the moment. If you still hold the same opinion after you've calmed down, then think of a tactful and non-confrontational way to approach the issue. You should and can communicate with your husband, but never attack him. It will only make him defensive. I realize that this is easier said than done. It takes practice and patience to catch things before they fly out of your mouth. The quicker you begin to master this skill, the more peaceful your home will be.

2. PUT YOURSELF IN HIS SHOES — LITERALLY. Go and find a pair of his shoes and stand in them. Not only will it start to calm you down because of how silly you feel, but stand there and think about things from his point of view — or his shoes! No matter how much you want things to be your way, you need to consider your husband's feelings, desires and life-long routines. It's an adjustment for him, too. It's not easy to change the way you do things overnight. Especially if you like the way things were. Be smart here. You love your husband for who he is. Don't ask him to change all of his quirky habits just to please you. It's important and comforting to mix some of the old with the new when you get married. Think about things from his point of view before you go inflicting yours on him.

Do Listen to Each Other

Actually, you'll want to do more than listen; hear what your partner is saying to you. I mean this in more ways than one. There are two "not-listening pitfalls" that can quickly cause serious damage to your relationship. They are:

NOT-LISTENING PITFALL NO. 1: ATTACK OF THE "YES, DEAR"

It's so easy to fall into the routine of "yessing" each other. *"Honey, I need you to waa, waa, waa, waa…"* He might hear the first few words then they fade out and sound like the adults on the Charlie Brown "Peanuts" cartoon. Next thing you know, he's giving you the ever popular "Yes, Dear" and has no clue about what he's just agreed to do.

As much as I hate to admit it, we wives fall victim to the "Yes, Dear" pitfall, too. Sometimes it's just easier to pass off a good "Yes, Dear" when he tries to ask you if you called his mother back and you're 45 minutes deep into watching *Grey's Anatomy*.

Don't do it. I know it's tempting and maybe what he's asking is not going to end world hunger; however, if you start this behavior with little things now, it can lead to bigger things and break down communication in your relationship.

If you notice that this is something that your husband does, bring it to his attention. If he doesn't get it and change his behavior, take the initiative and change yours. It may be difficult in the beginning, but over time you will clearly be able to tell when your husband is just "yessing" you or if he really means it. When you know it's happening, stop the conversation. Take responsibility for your role in it, and don't ask him questions when he is clearly preoccupied with something else. Likewise, if he tries to talk to you while you are desperately trying to find out how to make Rachael Ray's latest concoction on *30 Minute Meals*, kindly ask him to wait just a few minutes until the next commercial break when you can give him your full attention.

NOT LISTENING PITFALL NO. 2: HEARING WHAT YOU WANT TO HEAR

This pitfall is equally as dangerous as the first one, only this time you are giving him your full attention. But you are still not listening. You are only hearing what you want to hear. Men and women are different — period! We look, act, think and communicate differently. Realizing this could save you a lot of time and frustration.

When your husband tells you that he's not in the mood to eat spaghetti for dinner and asks if there something else, it doesn't mean that he secretly thinks your spaghetti tastes worse than eating worms and can't bear to suffer through it again! It simply means that he's not in the mood for spaghetti. Unless your cooking is really that atrocious, it's probably that simple.

Be open to hearing the words that are actually coming out of his mouth. Put down your super-duper decoder kit and don't assume there's more to it than what he's saying. Most men are truly not that complicated. So often we just skip right past the obvious and don't hear what he is simply saying to us. As women, we look deeper, for some secret message or hidden meaning; yet if we simply listen to what he is saying, we could cut out a lot of arguments, torment, and, yes, drama.

Don't Take Each Other for Granted

You've got him now. Your husband, plus a sparkly new ring, his last name, and the image of him tearfully pledging his undying love for you on a nicely packaged DVD that you can watch over and over with the simple click of a button. In addition, knowing that you two are bound together for the rest of your lives should be comforting. But don't cross the line from being comfortable to being complacent.

Just because you signed a marriage license, it doesn't give you license to take him for granted. When you live together day in and day out, it's very easy to get used to some of the things your husband may do for you. To expect him to do things and become unappreciative as though he *has* to do them can be extremely detrimental to your marriage.

There's no law saying that your husband has to call you if he is going to be home late from work. Should he? Yes, but does he *have* to? No. Your husband did not vow to put air in your tires when they are low or pledge to be the resident bug killer, but chances are that he does these things anyway. They might seem small and easy to overlook, but they are some of the best perks about having a husband and living together.

Next time your husband takes your car and comes back with an oil change, stop and appreciate it. Whatever nice thing your husband may do, acknowledge it by thanking him and recognize how sweet it is. Remember when you two were dating and he went that extra mile? It gave you that warm and fuzzy feeling when he sent flowers, planned surprise dinners, or gave you that special gift. I'm not going to lie; very few husbands keep these things up on a regular basis. Flowers start to come less frequently — on Valentine's Day, your birthday, or if he's really in the doghouse. Surprises might dwindle, too, and the special gifts... well, those come in different packages. Instead of the Tiffany charm bracelet, you get your computer software updated. Or your car washed and waxed after a rainy day. Or even better, you have a shoulder to cuddle up on after a heart-tugging episode of *Law and Order*. These are your warm and fuzzy moments now. Appreciate whatever special little things your husband does to take care of you and know that it is one of the many ways he may show his love for you.

Also, know that it's a two-way street. If he starts taking you for granted, stop taking his shirts to the dry-cleaners. He'll start to notice that they do not miraculously get up out of the hamper, become clean, and then hang themselves, all neatly wrapped in plastic, back in the closet. Or don't remind him that it's his mother's birthday and let him deal with that colossal guilt trip on his own. He'll definitely get a wake-up call. I'm not suggesting that you maliciously play games with your husband, but sometimes we all need a little reminder of just how good we have it.

Do Be Considerate When You're Decorating

Another helpful hint for you to keep in mind as you are setting up your new home is that it's his home, too! You are sharing this space with someone you love. *Both* of you should be as comfortable in it as possible. Ladies, if he tells you that he doesn't care what you do when you're decorating, don't take him literally. It does not give you a license to fill up the whole house with pink flowers. Again, you have to remember that it is his home, too. Unless your man is a big decorating buff (just because he watches *Extreme Makeover: Home Edition* with you doesn't make him an interior designer), chances are he's going to leave most of the finishing touches to you.

He may want to help pick out the big things like couches, the bedroom set and, of course, the electronics and let you deal with the drapes, plants, pictures and throw pillows. Just know that too much lace, frill or flowers will make him cringe every time he walks through the front door.

Well, he said he doesn't care. True, but that was probably the easiest thing to say to avoid having to spend the afternoon in Ikea picking out forks, bathmats and toothbrush holders.

Now is a good time to step back into his shoes. Think about his taste and the things that he likes. If he has no taste, maybe he has a favorite color. I can guarantee you it's not pink. Try to find things that you like, and that he'll like, too.

Always run things past him to make sure he's comfortable with your choice. Not because you have to, but because it's his home, too. Pay attention and learn his cues. Show him what you've picked out and ask for his opinion. But don't give him five striped patterns for the dining room curtains and expect him to pick one. Just show him the one you really want, or two at the most, then see if he has a reaction to it. Some men really just don't care. Some will voice their true opinion. If you can't read your husband yet, don't worry over time it will come. Now don't mistake this for mind-reading; you can never assume you know what he is thinking. However, certain things like judging which throw pillows he'll like, you should be able to safely tell.

And finally, make sure your home represents both of you. At least all of the neutral common areas, like the kitchen, living room, bedroom, etc. Make sure that the little personal touches tie in both of your likes. Don't put five 8x10 framed photos of your family on the mantle and one 4x6 of his. If he likes jazz, utilize it in the artwork you choose. Small touches can strengthen a marriage in big ways. The fact that you thought of him and his interests, and care that he is happy will make you the wife he brags about — rather than being a reason he complains.

Do Share the Household Chores

Who wants to do chores? The word "chores" itself even sounds daunting.

Some people are neat freaks and some surround themselves with clutter and mess. Some people say that cleaning relaxes them (I'd like to meet those people and invite them over to relax at my house), and some people get a knot in their back at the thought of picking up a broom.

Regardless of whether you like them or not, chores need to be done. And they are much easier to handle if you do not take them all on yourself. Just because you are the wife, doesn't mean that you are Katie, Katie the cleaning lady, too! You and your husband need to break them up however it works for the two of you, but make sure both of you have something to do!

The best way to make sure that you are not the only one on cleaning duty is to have a discussion about chores from the beginning. Don't attack him with all of the things you are not going to do. Instead, sit down with a pen and paper and list all of the chores that need to be done. If you live in a house, don't forget the outside chores, too. Then start divvying them up. Alternate picking who will do what and begin by choosing the things you won't mind doing first. It is important to keep in mind that everything may not need to be even-steven. You might have more chores on your list, but his chores might include harder labor or be more time-consuming like cutting the grass.

In fact, if dividing up chores one by one seems too tedious, you can always split them up in groups. For instance, Napoleon is responsible for the garage and the outside of the house, and I pretty much tackle the inside. We make exceptions and help each other out on special occasions and when one of us just needs a little help. It works out pretty well, except for the year that he had a lawn man, and I didn't have a cleaning service, but we won't go there.

Next, you need to agree on some kind of schedule for when the chores will be done. It doesn't have to be written down and posted on the refrigerator, we're not in kindergarten anymore, but it gives both of you an idea of when things will be completed. If it helps, tell him that if you know he's going to vacuum every Saturday morning, you won't ask him all the time when it's going to be done. More than likely he'll be very happy to agree.

Cleaning toilets, emptying a trashcan filled with tampons, and wiping razor stubble out of the sink are all very personal and, depending who you ask, might be considered nasty chores to do. You and your husband have to figure out how you want to handle them or, trust me, unless you married Mr. Clean (thumbs up to you lucky ladies), you'll be the one doing all of them.

Don't Harp on Silly Stuff

Who cares if the toilet seat is up or down, or if the cap is on the toothpaste? Get a grip, or your own toothpaste, and let the gripe go!

It's so cliché to even address some of these stereotypical gripes, so I'll be really brief. Life is too short to give the toilet seat so much of your precious time. Once you get into your marriage, you'll realize that there are bigger fish to fry, hills to climb, battles to pick (since I'm being cliché, why not go there?), and that it really doesn't make much difference if he lowers the toilet seat or not. The following is probably the simplest piece of advice that I can give: if you go to use the bathroom and he left the toilet seat up... put it down.

It used to drive me crazy when Napoleon would come home from work, step out of his pants, and leave them on the floor of our walk-in closet. I just knew it was the end of the free world! I tried to figure out how I was going to tell him to pick his pants up without sounding like a nag. Then I stopped thinking about me, me, me and I put myself in his shoes, or in this case his pants. OK, but seriously, I thought about how he might feel. Maybe it would drive him crazy that he can't step out of his pants and leave them on the floor. After all, it is *his* closet, too. *His* house, too. If he can't leave *his* pants on the floor of *his* closet in *his* house, where else could he possibly have the freedom to leave them? After thinking about it like that, his pants on the floor suddenly didn't seem so serious. Most of the time, I don't even notice his pants anymore. If I see them on the floor and feel the need, I pick them up and drop them in the hamper. If not, after a day or two — amazingly, he picks them up himself.

Living Together: Do's and Don'ts

DON'T START HABITS YOU DON'T PLAN ON KEEPING. If you get up every morning the first month you're married and make your husband an omelet and hand-squeezed orange juice, you better believe he's going to expect it every day.

DON'T AVOID DOING NICE THINGS BECAUSE YOU'RE SCARED YOU'RE STARTING HABITS YOU DON'T PLAN ON KEEPING. Learn the difference, and make him that breakfast every once in a while. It's a loving thing to do.

DO KEEP THE SYSTEMS THAT YOU TWO HAVE BUILT BEFORE MARRIAGE IF THEY ALREADY WORK FOR BOTH OF YOU. Don't go changing things that work just because you got married and you're a little emotional.

DO BE FLEXIBLE. Try something. If it doesn't work, talk about it and change things. That's the beauty of spending the rest of your life with someone. You have plenty of time to figure things out.

DON'T DO THINGS THAT YOU REALLY DON'T WANT TO DO. It brings frustration, resentment and turmoil to your relationship.

DO CREATE YOUR OWN SPACE. Everyone needs some space to retreat to and call their own — even married people.

DO TRY AND MAKE SURE HE HAS HIS OWN ROOM. Be it a garage or an extra bedroom, every man needs his own room where he can play video games, watch sports, work on the computer, or do whatever he likes to do.

DON'T BOTHER HIM ABOUT THE WAY HE KEEPS HIS ROOM. As long as there are no living things growing in there, let him be. Besides, we pretty much run the rest of the house, anyway.

DON'T PROTEST HIS "UGLY CHAIR." Every man has an "ugly" something that he wants in the house. Fighting him on it only makes him want it more. Work with him to find a spot for it where it won't be an eyesore for you.

DO EAT TOGETHER. Breakfast, lunch or dinner. One of them or all of them, just make sure you share a meal!

DO TALK ABOUT HAVING PETS BEFORE YOU MOVE IN TOGETHER. Pets are like having kids. You both have to be ready for them before you bring them home!

DO BE CONSIDERATE IF YOU ALREADY HAVE A PET. Your four cats or his German Shepherd may have to find a new place to sleep. You two have each other to cozy up to now.

DO CHECK WITH EACH OTHER BEFORE INVITING PEOPLE OVER. You wouldn't want him to bring his buddy home from work to find you lying on the couch in your bra and panties, would you?

DON'T FIGHT OVER THE REMOTE CONTROL. Let him hold it; men like to think that they are in control — but decide on the television show together.

DO BE CONSIDERATE OF EACH OTHER'S BEDTIMES. Don't start cleaning out your dresser when he normally goes to sleep.

DO GO TO BED TOGETHER. At least sometimes, it's nice to end the day with your husband by your side.

DO DECIDE WHO GETS TO SHOWER FIRST IN THE MORNING *BEFORE* YOU GO TO BED. Set up a morning routine so you both can be on time.

DO SHOWER TOGETHER. It's nice to have somebody wash your back… and other places, too.

DO SAY, "I LOVE YOU" EVERY DAY. Life is short; make sure your partner knows how much you care.

DO HUG. Just because it feels good.

Don't forget to touch each other. A stroke on the face, fingers through the hair, and a pat on the butt go a long way.

Do say, "I'm sorry." If you're wrong and you know it, fess up.

Do forgive him. Unless it's one of the seven deadly sins, forgive him. Everyone makes mistakes.

Do talk about current events. Stay up on what's going on in the world, and share your views with each other.

Do laugh together. Every day, several times a day.

Do know what makes him happy. A big juicy steak, playing flag football in the park, making love to you. You should know what makes your husband happy and do your best to keep him that way.

Do learn each other's favorites. Foods, colors, places, songs, people, and sodas... everything that your spouse loves.

Do appreciate his interests. You don't have to like them, but respect them... as long as they're respectable.

Don't lie to your husband. Do you really need a reason why?

Do kiss the mirror with red lipstick sometimes when you leave. It's sexy and exciting to leave little hints of love around the house.

DO LEAVE HIM NOTES IN HIS BRIEFCASE. Tease him with all the naughty things you can't wait to do with him later that night. Just make sure none of his coworkers have access to his bag.

DO SLEEP IN TOGETHER AT LEAST ONE MORNING A MONTH. Everybody is so busy, but make the time to snuggle, cuddle and (if you're lucky) have some morning sex with your partner.

DO PLAY HOOKY FROM WORK TOGETHER. Every once in a while, call in sick and spend the day in bed playing doctor.

DO UNDERSTAND THAT EVERYBODY HAS A BAD DAY SOMETIMES. Attitudes come up, and may be about many things besides you. Ignore this as long as it doesn't happen often.

DON'T TAKE YOUR BAD DAY OUT ON YOUR SPOUSE. He's not the one who pissed you off, so why do it to him?

Wives' Words

ABOUT LIVING TOGETHER

"Whatever habits existed before the marriage will be there afterwards. Don't expect too much change. If he was a slob the night before the ceremony, he will be that same slob the next morning."

—CHERYL, MARRIED FIVE YEARS

"Don't project yourself onto your spouse and get mad if he doesn't do it your way (cleaning up, cooking, paying bills). Work it out and figure out who likes (doesn't mind) doing what."

—ROBIN, MARRIED SIX YEARS

"You will be exposed to habits that will annoy the hell out of you. You can nag about everything, but that will be a total drag — for you and for him! If your husband, no matter how many times you ask him, never seems to be able to put a new toilet paper roll in the bathroom, then it may be better for your sanity to just know that you'll be the toilet paper replacer in the family."

—NANCY, MARRIED TWO YEARS

"Be very careful; living together is different than being married. We lived together a year before getting married, and it was amazing... we still did not skip the one year situations that have to be worked out. Marriage is a totally different creature."

—RACHEL, MARRIED 12 YEARS

This can be a challenge, making 'yours' and 'mine' into 'ours.' My advice would simply be to be open to change and if necessary learn to love that ugly favorite chair, painting, 49rs pillow (whatever 'it' may "be). Set some ground rules as to what is expected as far as grocery shopping, cooking, cleaning, laundry, etc. A lot of assumptions are made about who is doing what."

—ALLISON, MARRIED 12 YEARS

"Being compatible helps and also respectful the way any roommate should act." —SHARON, MARRIED EIGHT YEARS

"Try to really be honest about who you are, and your beliefs before you move in together. It is a lot easier to deal with major differences if you don't feel like someone has done a Dr. Jekyll and Mr. Hyde on you — just to get you in." —HOPE, MARRIED 14 YEARS

"Be patient." —NDIDI, MARRIED SIX YEARS

"Your home should be a place of solitude and relaxation when you both come home from a long day's work."

—MONICA, MARRIED THREE YEARS

WHAT WAS THE HARDEST CHALLENGE DURING YOUR FIRST YEAR OF MARRIAGE?

"Cooking."   —WANDA, MARRIED NINE YEARS

"Sharing responsibility for household expenses."
                                                   —TOMIKA, MARRIED THREE YEARS

"Deciding where to go during the holidays — my family or his."
                                                   —NDIDI, MARRIED SIX YEARS

"Really getting on the same page with my husband in perceiving us as a family, as life partners. It's a real transition to go from the mentality of dating to actually being married... I think both of us being in our mid-thirties also made it more challenging because we were accustomed to doing things certain ways before, so it took some time to adjust. I had a lot of 'are we gonna make it?' thoughts."
                                                   —NANCY, MARRIED TWO YEARS

"Getting my husband to realize I was not his mother or grandmother. Just because they did something didn't mean I thought I should be doing that too."
                                                   —RACHEL, MARRIED 12 YEARS

"Learning that I didn't have to be 'Miss Independent' anymore."
                                                   —MONICA, MARRIED THREE YEARS

"The hardest challenge for me was communication. I was accustomed to keeping things inside, feeling and emotions were rarely discussed."
                                                   —CHERYL, MARRIED FIVE YEARS

"The reality of 'our' finances. The two becoming one was really difficult for us. Some days, it still is (a dozen years later)."
—ALLISON, MARRIED 12 YEARS

"Getting accustomed to having to answer to someone else and consider their time, feelings, etc."
—RHONDA, MARRIED 20 YEARS

"The hardest thing so far has been exercising patience while we work through, what seems to be, all of the moving parts right now."
—JENNIFER, MARRIED FOUR MONTHS

"Getting to really know my husband... When they say that 'you don't really know someone until you live with them,' it's really true."
—HOPE, MARRIED 14 YEARS

"When you are married, you cannot just walk away. Especially during the first year, you are actually under more pressure to work it out. Compromise and sacrifice is essential in the first year of marriage."
—QUISA, MARRIED ONE YEAR

5

Sex? Sex. Sex!

THE NEWLYWED MYTHS –
LOTS, LITTLE, OR LACK OF

Sex. It's a very touchy subject — literally. Most newlyweds believe that once they cross the threshold into their honeymoon suite, they'll be all over each other like two horny teenagers in the back of a movie theater. Not only is it assumed that you'll "do it" every second of your honeymoon, but the whole first year of marriage, too. You're newlyweds, aren't you? Well, for those of you who can miraculously make this happen, kudos to you! You may as well skip to the next chapter. But, for the majority of us who get tired just thinking about it, please keep reading.

Napoleon and I got married on a beautiful Saturday morning. Our reception was in the afternoon and we planned a big after-party for that evening in our hotel suite. By the time our wedding day came, I was running purely on adrenaline and fumes. I was so tired from the previous months of planning, worrying and built-up excitement, I just knew I was going to crash before the night was through. I told Napoleon that if we were going to consummate our marriage on our wedding day, which we really wanted to do, we would have to do so before our after-party or we both would be very disappointed. So we asked our friends to give us some space, and I'm sure you can figure what happened next.

Later that night, after greeting and celebrating with our closest friends at our after-party, I was curled up on the bed enjoying some of the hardest and most well-deserved sleep of my life. I probably could have slept the whole next week, too, but we still had brunch with the family on Sunday morning, some last minute shopping, and we needed to be on a plane headed for Mexico first thing Monday morning. Was I about to get any more rest? No. But did I feel like I still needed to uphold one of the most popular newlywed sex myths? Yes. Did I uphold it? I wish!

The reality is, Napoleon and I had an amazing honeymoon, almost too good to be true. We slept, we partied, we slept, we rode bikes, we slept, we sunbathed on the beach, we slept, and yes, we had sex. Was it every day, every second? No. But, more importantly, was it enough and satisfying to us? Yes. And that should be what's important to you, too. Is your sex life enough for both of you, and is it satisfying to both of you? If it is and you have sex once a day, that's fine. If it is and you have sex once a week, that's fine, too. There's no newlywed sex committee hiding under your bed to judge you, and there are no newlywed standards that you have to meet.

Your sex life will most likely go through highs and lows. If you're on a high on your honeymoon, enjoy it; just don't panic if you go into a low when you get back home — with a little work and attention it will peak back around. The same thing goes if you are on a low during your honeymoon — know that you can get that high back and take advantage of the extra sleep.

Over the long term, the important thing will be to remain creative and do things to keep your sex-life interesting. For instance, plan a romantic evening of lovemaking and greet your husband naked when he comes home from work. Watch videos, play games, have a quickie in the morning, and try new things. Just make sure that you and your husband are having fun. Sex is like any other part of your relationship; you have to *work* at it to make it great. Fortunately, this is the kind of work that I don't mind doing.

Don't Believe the Myths

There are three common myths that instantly come to mind when newlywed, marriage or sex are mentioned in the same sentence.

1. Myth #1: Newlyweds have sex every waking hour of their honeymoon.

2. Myth #2: Newlyweds have sex all the time during their first year of marriage.

3. Myth #3: Married couples never have sex.

They may be widely known ideas, but don't buy into them. They're not facts — hence that's why we call them myths. Actually, the activity in your sex life has less to do with your marital status — unless you were waiting until you said, "I do" — and more to do with the dynamics of your relationship and your sex drives and desires. Yes, the high of getting married can enhance your desire or the stress of getting married can deflate it, but both circumstances are only temporary.

Newlyweds have sex every waking hour of their honeymoon...

Yeah, right. I already discussed this myth earlier in the chapter, but it's worth addressing some more. First, as a bride, don't be surprised if you spend the first few days of your honeymoon recuperating from the wedding and the months of intense planning. Physically and mentally, there's a good chance that you will be simply exhausted.

Yes, the pressure to perform on your honeymoon can be intense. Who is putting this pressure on you? Are you supposed to go home and give an oral report to your friends and family about how many times you did it, where, and who was on top? Absolutely not! Your sex life should be between you and your husband. And you should have sex as often or as infrequently as you and your husband want. Sex during your honeymoon is supposed to be fun and spontaneous, not something you put on your checklist of things to do: water-ski, tour Mayan ruins, bike-ride into town, have sex for the second time today. That's just silly — but possibly a good tactic to keep the fire burning later in your relationship. If you and your husband have high sex drives and don't leave the room until dinner, enjoy it. If you and your husband don't wake up until dinner, enjoy that too. You just got married; don't worry about trying to keep up with the Joneses. Chances are they're recuperating, too.

Newlyweds have sex all the time during their first year of marriage...

Who started this myth? Must've been a man with a whole lot of stamina or a woman with a whole lot of K-Y Jelly. It's just not true. This myth goes hand-in-hand with the "*You must be so happy*" line. Happy and sexin'. That is what you are led to believe when you first get married. You're happy and you're having sex.

I joke about this lightly. I hope you are happy, and I hope you and your husband are having sex. But, realistically, all 365 days of your first year won't be blissful, and they won't be spent pleasing each other either. There are so many emotions (fear, intimidation, inadequacy) and challenges (moving in together, in-laws, establishing your roles) that you deal with during the first year of marriage that even the most sexual person might not want to have sex all the time.

I must refer back to my main point about sex in marriage. You should have as little or as much sex as you and your husband are comfortable and happy with. Now, in no way am I advising or encouraging you not to have sex — it is a vital part of marriage — I just want to dispel the myth that there must be an overabundance of sex during the first year, and make it clear that you are perfectly normal if you are not acting like jack-rabbits every day.

Married couples never have sex

This is one of men's biggest fears. And it sounds pretty scary to me, too. Thank goodness, it's not true. Of course, married couples have sex. Are there some who don't? I suppose so, but being married does not equate to losing your sex life. Can it happen? Yes, and that's why like many other areas of your marriage, you have to work at your sex life. Like anything else, if you don't pay attention to it, love it, take care of it, and keep it thriving, it will stop working.

Sex might come easier for some and be more challenging for others. There is no right or wrong amount as long as you and your husband are in sync and happy. Still, if you're not happy, you are not alone. Many couples seek some sort of sex therapy or counseling from a professional. It can be a helpful option if you and your husband are having difficulty communicating or finding the right balance in your sex life.

It's important to create a sex life that is satisfying to both of you — but only for the good of the two of you. It doesn't matter what your best friend thinks, what his boys say, or what society dictates (like these three deceptive myths). All that matters is that you have one — a sex life, that is — and that you and your husband are satisfied with it.

Do Keep the Romance Alive

There is another popular newlywed sex myth that bears an honorable mention: *The romance dies after marriage.* One way to ensure that you keep romantic gestures flowing is to practice what you preach.

Let me set the scene. You and three of your closest girl-friends are sitting in a booth at your favorite girls-night-out spot sipping martinis and swapping stories — or shall I say frustrations — about your wonderful husbands.

"*He used to want to have sex every night,*" one says. "*I know, my husband couldn't walk by me without touching me; now he barely makes eye contact,*" another chimes in. "*He couldn't keep his hands off me when we would curl up on the couch and watch movies. He's also gained a few pounds, and he always wears his holey old lucky college T-shirt when we're lounging around the house. He's just not romantic anymore. He doesn't do any of the things he used to do before we got married."*

OK, stop right there. I'm sure we've all made or heard some of these common complaints before. Many times we are so quick to point out what he is not doing, instead of looking at what we're not doing. Instead we need to take ownership of the part that we may play in the scenario and work for what we want. Are you still doing some of the things to spark the romance that you did before you got married? Chances are you've put more effort into getting all dolled up for drinks with the ladies than you have into hanging out with your husband. After all, he's your husband, you've got him now, right? Yes and no. He is your husband and you do have him now, but if you want to keep him and your sex life exciting, you still need to keep *you* exciting, too. At least sometimes!

I talked about staying a hot chick in Chapter Three, and that can directly affect your sex life. I'm not suggesting that you have to be picture perfect all the time. Most husbands would be willing to have sex with you if you were wearing a head scarf, mud-mask and a burlap sack. However, if you desire a little more romantic foreplay and not just sex, you have to practice what you preach. For example, you don't want him to wear the same ratty T-shirt every night, but you're walking around the house in extra-large granny panties all the time. True, they may be more comfortable, but they're not going to get the party started.

Take the initiative and set the tone. If you want attention, attract it in how you look, act and feel. Think back to your pre-engagement days when you first started dating. Dig into your old bag of tricks and makeup bag, too! If you lose the mud-mask and period panties for some lip-gloss and a sexylace thong, and he doesn't stop, drop and roll, then feel free to bitch to your girlfriends. OK seriously, in most cases, a little initiative, a positive attitude, and some cleavage is all it takes to keep your man's advances coming. But if that extra effort is not working, bitching to your girlfriends won't help. Instead, try talking to him. He might be overworked, stressed with a family problem, or have some other serious outside distraction. Whatever the cause may be, addressing the dilemma lovingly and supportively is the best way to resolve it.

Sex! Sex. Sex?: Do's and Don'ts

DO TAKE TIME TO CREATE THE SEX LIFE YOU WANT. You have your whole life to build your sex life. That's why it's called a sex *life*.

DO KEEP YOUR SEX LIFE INTERESTING. There's nothing worse than boring sex… except more boring sex.

DON'T DO ANYTHING THAT YOU'RE NOT COMFORTABLE WITH. Married or not — period.

DO WHAT MAKES YOU FEEL SEXY. Wear pretty panties, shave your legs, and shower yourself with fragrant body wash. Take the time to do the things that make you feel sexy.

DO HAVE SEX IN EVERY ROOM OF YOUR HOUSE. Why not?

Do USE YOUR ASSETS TO HELP YOU GET WHAT YOU WANT. Women were blessed with beautiful bodies to make men weak. Well, maybe not to make them weak, but still this is the one area where you can use what you've got to get what you want.

Do HAVE A NOONER. Meet at home for lunch... and skip the lunch!

Do PAT HIM ON THE BUTT WHEN HE WALKS BY. Every once in a while, you've got to let him know that he's still got it.

Do LEAVE THE LIGHTS ON. Men are visual people. He'd much rather feel *and* see, too.

Do WATCH DIRTY MOVIES TOGETHER. How taboo... and fun!

Don't BE EMBARRASSED. Get over it and get adventurous. He's your husband now.

Don't BE A PRUDE. See above.

Do ASK YOUR HUSBAND WHAT HE LIKES. Find out what pleases him and share what pleases you, too. Find out if he wants you in high heels and handcuffs, or in silk and slippers.

Do EXPERIMENT WITH SEX TOYS AND GAMES. There's a wide assortment of fun and safe toys and games available to enhance your sex life. Spice it up and have some fun.

DO SURPRISE HIM BY WEARING A NEW PIECE OF LIN-GERIE. Keep your lingerie drawer stocked with cute and current items.

DO DANCE FOR HIM. Seduce him. Tease him. Strip for him. And don't let him touch you until you're done. Talk about driving him crazy.

DO START YOUR DAY OFF WITH A QUICKIE. A little morning sex can make for a great day.

DO SAY NO WHEN YOU DON'T FEEL LIKE DOING IT. Sex when you're not interested is worse than saying no.

DON'T ALWAYS SAY NO WHEN YOU DON'T FEEL LIKE DOING IT. Sometimes you gotta suck it up and say yes, when you really feel like rolling over, curling up, and saying no. Chances are you'll enjoy it once you get started.

DO EXPECT HIM TO SAY NO SOMETIMES, TOO. Believe it or not, this rare occurrence does happen. Don't make a big deal about it; he'll probably wake you in the morning for a quickie.

Wives' Words

About Sex

"Don't use sex as a weapon or a punishment. Let him know you desire and need him sexually. Have fun; don't be afraid to be his freak in the bedroom. He will love you for it."
— RACHEL, MARRIED 12 YEARS

"He should always want it from you. The day he stops desiring you, start asking questions."
— CHERYL, MARRIED FIVE YEARS

"Sex is important, but intimacy is just as important. Try and maintain a balance of both, but one without the other doesn't work."
— ROBIN, MARRIED SIX YEARS

"In some ways, sex is better because you are so much less inhibited with your husband... you may be more relaxed and comfortable with trying new things. Have sex in unexpected places. Make the first move. Role play. The biggest thing is making the effort because you may not feel like it a lot of the time."
— NANCY, MARRIED TWO YEARS

"Sex should be as good to you as it is to your husband, so hopefully you are enjoying it too! If not, communicate your wants, needs, and desires to your husband."
— MONICA, MARRIED THREE YEARS

"Offer it up cheerfully. May sound easy for the newlyweds but, whether you believe it or not, there will come a day when it may not be that easy."
— ALLISON, MARRIED 12 YEARS

"Don't rely on spontaneity — especially after kids."

—RHONDA, MARRIED 20 YEARS

"Sex is better away from home, so go away a lot! Get away from chores and tasks and piles of laundry."

—SHARON, MARRIED EIGHT YEARS

"We talk openly and OFTEN about sex. Flirt with your husband, tease him, keep him guessing, and keep him interested. To keep the sex in your marriage, stay sexy!"

—JENNIFER, MARRIED FOUR MONTHS

"Have lots of it, as often as possible. Don't ever stop loving sex; make the same commitment to it that you do to your marriage. It is truly one of the greatest things in marriage."

—HOPE, MARRIED 14 YEARS

"Don't be stingy with it or use it as a source of control... If you're bored, maybe he is too. Talk about what you like and don't like."

—ANGELA, MARRIED 16 YEARS

6

Money –
Mine, Yours, and Ours

BALANCING LOVE, MARRIAGE,
AND THE CHECKBOOK

Balancing love, marriage, and money can be as difficult as balancing your checkbook; and yes, you have to do both. You promised to love him for better or for worse, for richer or for poorer, remember? Well, when you said those vows, you became legally and financially tied to each other. That includes everything you both do — individually or together — from that precious day forward. You both still have your own credit scores, your own bank accounts, and your own growing pile of debt, but if the unthinkable were to happen to your new husband, guess who would be responsible for his part? That's right — you would.

I don't say that to scare you, but we live in the real world where you should be prepared for anything, especially when it comes to money. It's extremely important for you to set up a plan, preferably in the beginning of your marriage, for how you and your husband will handle your finances. Options include setting up separate accounts, joint accounts, or separate *and* joint accounts; letting him do the bills, having you do the bills, having the two of you alternate, or doing them together. There are many approaches and you have to find the one that works best for both of you.

There are many positive things that you can do to make sure that you and your hubby stay happy and rolling in the dough. Talk about it. Keep the lines of communication open. Set up a weekly or monthly meeting to discuss your finances. Ask questions or read up on things that you don't know about. Stocks, mutual funds, and 401K plans can all seem very confusing, but don't be afraid to learn what's going on with your money and how to make it grow.

Don't take on the responsibility of handling the money if you're no good at it. You shouldn't be in charge of the checkbook if you have a compulsive shopping disorder. And don't force your husband to do it if he is not good at this. Let's hope one of you will want to do it, *and* will be good at it. If not, make sure you compromise and work through things together. And if you decide not to handle the money, make sure that you always know what's going on with it — always.

Why? Well, let's say — hypothetically, of course — that your husband handles all of the money in your relationship, everything from the bills to the investments to which bank you use. He gives you a platinum credit card and a checkbook and makes sure that every bill is paid on time. Sounds like there's nothing to worry about, right? Wrong! One day, on his way home from work, your husband might be involved in a life-threatening car accident. He could spend two months in the hospital and another two at home in bed recuperating. Even though your paychecks are still directly deposited into your bank account, you have no idea what to do with the checks, because you never asked him any questions about your finances. Perhaps it isn't until your cell phone gets temporarily disconnected that you even think about paying the bills. Fortunately, this story is not true for you, but it probably is for somebody.

Let's give your hypothetical situation a happy ending. All three of you recovered — you, your husband, and your checkbook. It is important to understand that this scenario could just as easily happen to men as well as women. Many women today make as much or more money than their spouses, and are responsible for the family's finances. If you take care of the household finances, protect your husband and yourself by showing him where you keep the financial records and the process that you use to handle them. If you don't manage the finances, ask your husband to walk you through his system one time. Remember, there is nothing wrong with one spouse handling the money if that's what works in your relationship, as long as *both* of you take the time to understand them.

Money can be intimidating, whether you're married or single. It's one of the leading causes of arguments between married couples, but it doesn't have to be for you and your husband. Talk to each other, devise a plan, set up a budget, and make a conscious decision not to let money cause tension in your marriage. Then, break out your calculator, and get to balancing.

Do Know Your Money ABCDs

It's one thing to be financially irresponsible when you're single, but it can create twice as many problems and double the amount of debt when there are two of you. You need to know what I call the Money ABCDs to make sure that you and your husband keep your finances in order from the beginning of your marriage. Utilizing the Money ABCDs can help eliminate the stress and problems associated with money by enabling you to proactively take control of your finances and make sure that they are stable, growing, and working for you.

Dealing with money can be intimidating, but it can't be avoided. What you don't know can and will hurt you when it comes to money, so knowing the ABCDs are crucial.

Money ABCDs

Analyze your
Budget,
Credit Reports and FICO Scores, and
Debt.

Analyze Your Budget

In order to make sure that you're managing your money correctly, you will need to create a budget. A budget is the breakdown of how much money you have coming in and how much money you have allocated to your expenses (in other words, how much you have going out). Again, in order for you to make sure that you are balancing your finances, or better yet making them grow, you need to list everything coming in and everything going out to ensure that you are generating the income that you desire and spending it in the most efficient way.

I realize that many of us would rather have our entire bodies waxed (yikes!) than sit down and create a budget, but it must be done. There are no good excuses why you cannot make this happen. We live in the information age. There are countless books, websites, computer software and professional financial planners for you to consult with regarding any questions or concerns. I've taken the liberty to name some key expenses that should be included in your budget to get you started. They are:

INCOMING EXPENSES:
Your salary
Your husband's salary
Any other source of income
    (part-time jobs, investments, inheritance, lottery winnings — I can dream, can't I?)

OUTGOING EXPENSES:
Rent/mortgage
Car notes
Car insurance
Money for savings
Student loans
Food
Gas
Credit cards
Utilities/house bills
Cell phone

Fun/entertainment

Miscellaneous

> (birthday gifts, yearly car registration, traffic tickets, clothes shopping, etc.)

Analyze Your Credit Reports and FICO Scores

It's vital that you know what's on your credit reports, plus what your FICO scores are. It is also vital that you have this information about your husband, too. As I said earlier, once you legally took him for better or for worse, you also took him for well off or for broke, for no debt or for debt. Not only can you be held responsible for his financial actions from the beginning of your marriage, but his FICO scores can affect the interest rate of any major purchases you want to make together, like a house or a car.

Your credit report lists information about your financial history, including how many accounts you have, how you pay them (be it on time, 30 days late, 60 days late, etc.), or if you don't pay them at all. There are three credit bureaus (Experian, TransUnion, and Equifax) that most lenders refer to, hence you have three different FICO scores. Yes, it is imperative that you check all three credit reports. I know it sounds like a lot, but it is simple to get a copy of each and worth the money you could be saving by catching mistakes on the report or learning how to increase your score. Because all three bureaus are widely used and all three are entirely separate companies, you have to know what is on all of them.

What's on your report(s) determines your FICO score(s), so it is important to make sure that all of the information is accurate and updated. Most lenders determine how much they will lend you and at what interest rate by your FICO score. Created by the Fair Isaac Corporation, the score takes into account several factors including your payment history, how long you've had the credit, and how much you owe. The higher your FICO score the better. I have included several invaluable resources in the back of the book, including the websites for all three credit bureaus and the Fair Isaac Corporation. These websites explain more details about FICO scores, your credit reports, and how to make sure that yours are the best that they can be.

Analyze Your Debt

Once you have created your budget, have reviewed your credit reports, and know your FICO score, you can then analyze your debt. Hopefully you have little or no debt. However, if you're like most Americans who average approximately $8000 in credit card debit, you have some work to do. Look at your debt, accept that it's there, and then commit to getting rid of it.

Everyone's financial situation is different. Fortunately, there are several ways to pay off your debt; I suggest doing your research (you just planned the wedding of the century so don't tell me that you don' know how to do research!) or consult a professional financial advisor to determine the best way for your specific circumstances. Some options to explore are:

- Paying off the debt with the highest interest rate first, then moving to the next one until they are all paid off

- Consolidating your debt into one lump sum via a debt consolidation company
- Consolidating your debt onto one low-interest credit card
- Paying off your debt through a home equity loan

Don't Avoid Difficult Financial Conversations

I realize that many of you don't want to read about these things (the sex chapter is much more interesting) so I'll be quick and to the point. Just because you don't talk about something doesn't mean that it's not happening. When it comes to money, ignorance is not bliss. Ignorance can leave you, your new husband, and future children (gasp! that's a whole different book) in financial ruins.

Honestly, who really wants to talk about their will? Especially just after getting married. But death is perhaps the one thing that is guaranteed to all of us — whether you prepare for it or not. If you have not taken the surprisingly quick and easy steps to put a will in place or a living trust (you need to know the difference), and the unthinkable happens sooner than later, one of you could be faced with finances that are in shambles.

I've listed some often dreaded topics that may be necessary for discussion as you and your husband are responsibly laying your financial groundwork. After all, we all want to retire at forty-five, right? If they apply, make sure that you consider them in your planning. I've included several valuable resources in the back of the book to help you swiftly, knowledgeably and painlessly tackle these unpopular but necessary issues.

TOPICS FOR DISCUSSION:

- 401K plans/Retirement plans
- Investments
- Taxes
- Disability insurance
- Life insurance
- Will/Living trust
- Previous child's support
- Ex-wife's alimony payments

Money – Mine, Yours and Ours: Do's and Don'ts

DON'T MISTAKE MONEY FOR POWER. Confusing the two in a relationship can lead to its end.

DO TALK ABOUT MONEY. Discuss your plans, your goals, and your fears. Communication is essential.

DO THE WORK IT TAKES TO KEEP YOUR MONEY STRAIGHT AND YOUR RELATIONSHIP HAPPY. Read books, hire a financial consultant, and talk with your husband.

DON'T PRETEND THAT YOU KNOW IT ALL. There are hundreds of books that can help with money. Take the time to research them.

DON'T COUNT PENNIES. "*I made this much; you made that much.*" That is very dangerous territory. Never use how much you earn against each other.

DON'T EXPECT EVERYTHING TO BE EQUAL. You are in a partnership now. Sometimes you do more, sometimes your partner will do more. That's the beauty of having a partner.

DO CONSULT WITH HIM BEFORE YOU MAKE ANY MAJOR FINANCIAL DECISIONS. You may make your own money, but legally you two are tied together now. What you do affects him, too.

DO BE FLEXIBLE AND EXPECT YOUR INITIAL BUDGET TO CHANGE FOR A WHILE. It takes some time to work out the kinks. However, once you find what works, you can make necessary adjustments every six months or so.

DO HAVE A SYSTEM FOR SPENDING YOUR MONEY. Neither one of you should spend over $100, $500, or $1000 without discussing it first. Do whatever amount makes sense for you; just make sure that you have some sort of system.

DON'T JUST RUN DOWN TO THE BANK AND OPEN A JOINT ACCOUNT. Talk about it first, and make sure you have a good system in place. It's very easy to overdraw a joint account since both of you will have access to it.

DO REMEMBER TO BRING YOUR MARRIAGE LICENSE WITH YOU IF YOU DO DECIDE TO OPEN AN ACCOUNT TOGETHER. It's always wise to have your proof of marriage with you for your first year while you are still making changes to old accounts and opening new ones.

DON'T FORGET TO BRING MONEY TO OPEN THE AC-
COUNT. You can call your bank ahead of time and find
out how much you need to start.

DON'T ARGUE OVER CHECK STYLES. Compromise here,
and get the flowers and cute little babies on your personal
checks.

DO SAVE MONEY. Whether its $5 or $500, make sure you
save something, for the two of you, together.

DO SAVE EMERGENCY MONEY. Strive for at least three
months of bill money that you never touch.

DO KEEP A LITTLE ATTITUDE MONEY FOR YOU. Every
grown woman (and every grown man) needs some attitude money to splurge on something they normally
wouldn't buy.

DO MAKE SURE HE HAS SOME MONEY THAT HE DOESN'T
HAVE TO ACCOUNT FOR. How else is he going to surprise you with gifts and flowers?

DON'T RUB HIS NOSE IN BAD CREDIT. No matter how
much it stinks. Help him get back on track.

DO AVOID BUYING THINGS ON CREDIT. It's so tempting
to do, especially when you start to furnish your new place
together. Have a plan and use credit wisely and scarcely
or you will pay for it — literally — in the end.

Do pick a time to discuss your money and stick
     to it. Money discussions are usually dreaded, but it's
     easier if you have a schedule and an agenda to take care
     of business.

Do talk to your financial advisor about filing
     your taxes jointly or separately. There may be
     certain circumstances that make it beneficial to file taxes
     jointly or separately. Find out what's best for the two of
     you.

Wives' Words

About Money

"Money can be a HUGE issue. Figure out how you're going to handle money. Even if one person is in charge of the finances, make sure you are on the same page about what to do with your money. Allow the one not in charge to have some level of responsibility."
—Nancy, married two years

"I think everything should be shared (assets). If you have a hidden account, or something on the side, you're mentally setting yourself up for failure. If you wanted to be independently wealthy, you should have stayed single."
—Cheryl, married five years

"Understand each other's views on money (how to save, how to spend, what is important to each other) and work together to build a life that respects the other's spending habits."
—Robin, married six years

"Whoever handles money the best should manage the family money, but each person should have some money of their own that they are responsible for."
—Rachel, married 12 years

"When you marry someone, your money marries too. Sit down at least once a week and have a business meeting regarding finances. Too many marriages end in divorce due to money issues. It's no longer his paycheck, your paycheck; it's now one paycheck."
—Monica, married three years

"Share and communicate. SAVE, SAVE, SAVE!"
—ALLISON, MARRIED 12 YEARS

"Don't use it against each other... discuss major purchases before you buy anything." —SHARON, MARRIED EIGHT YEARS

"Over-communicate about money and be sure you're speaking the same language." —JENNIFER, MARRIED FOUR MONTHS

"Get as financially smart and free as you can before getting married. Become a team in making the two of you and your family financially free, and never hide anything from your spouse. They always find out." —HOPE, MARRIED 14 YEARS

"Get a joint account; pool your money together. You really must become one in order to make it work. Money has a way of becoming its own entity; it turns into a person that you fight over often." —WANDA, MARRIED NINE YEARS

"Keep separate accounts. If necessary, have a household account that you both can contribute to for household expenses. It keeps financial arguments down." —QUISA, MARRIED ONE YEAR

"First, talk, talk and talk until you're blue in the face about spending so you and your husband are on the same page. Second, keep a joint account for joint expenses and a separate account for you." —NDIDI, MARRIED SIX YEARS

7

Family and Friends 101

MANAGING INSTANT IN-LAWS, EXTENDED FAMILIES, AND FRIENDS

Before I got married, I considered my mother, my father and my sister to be my nuclear or immediate family — and they were before I got hitched. Now the man whom I vowed to love, cherish and honor is not just my lover and my friend, he is my family, too — my partner in my new nuclear family. When you married your husband you started a new family, too.

Guess what else you did? You instantly inherited your husband's entire family. Wow! That's a lot of family, a lot of feelings to deal with, and a lot more people to think about than you probably expected.

Inheriting all of these extra people can feel very overwhelming. Not only did they instantly become your family, but you are supposed to remember who all of them are, where they live, and how they are related. Unless you have a photographic memory or are really good at faking it at family parties, I suggest you make yourself a cheat sheet.

Your first lesson in Family and Friends 101 is to get yourself a notebook or a folder and write stuff down. Names, addresses, associations and other key things to remember. Sure, years from now, these strangers who act like they've known you all of your life will truly become like family. However, in the beginning, you have so much going on that it's easy to confuse Uncle John from Atlanta (who is really Cousin John from Suwannee) and Cousin Tom from Miami (who is really a long-time family friend from Upstate New York). Especially since the only time you met them was at your wedding, after the champagne toast and in the middle of your glazed-over I-just-got-married fog.

The second lesson in Family and Friends 101 is to be patient. Before you jump right in and start gossiping with his aunties, take a second to learn about everybody. There are a lot of family dynamics that you will have to sift through. The same auntie who swears she won't tell a soul how you really feel about your husband's sister could be the family big-mouth. You and your husband have enough work to do establishing your own relationship, so slow down and don't add to the drama by making relationships difficult with your in-laws. Be patient while building your relationships and understand that even though you instantly became family, it takes time for the love — or sometimes even the like — to grow.

Lesson Three in Family and Friends 101 is to recognize you are not the only person in this world with a mother, father, sister, brother, etc. He has a family, and chances are that the people in that family are just as important to him as yours are to you.

For example, the thought of having Thanksgiving dinner without your mother might seem absurd to you. On Thanksgiving, you've always known that you will get together with your family at your mother's house and eat a whole lot of good cookin'. Well, it's Thanksgiving for his family, too, complete with turkey, family and their own special traditions. Holidays like Thanksgiving might not be important to your husband, or he might have all of the same feelings about them and his family that you do about yours.

The Four C's that I discussed in Chapter Two (communication, compromise, commitment and creativity) are very useful in such stressful family situations and they should be called upon often. You are going to have to effectively communicate with your husband about what you are willing to creatively compromise on. It is very important to acknowledge and appreciate his relationship with his family, no matter how wonderful, or weird, they may be.

The fourth lesson in Family and Friends 101 is to realize that he'll have some friends that you absolutely love, and some that you wish would take a fishing expedition in South America — permanently! And chances are he will feel the same way about some of your friends. This is normal. Unless his friend is disrespectful, you should accept that their friendship is not ending (as annoying as that may be) and do your best to respect it. If the friend is disrespectful, your husband should swiftly put him in his place, and so should you if one of your girlfriends acts rude or behaves inappropriately in some other manner toward your husband. Also, do your best to avoid spending unnecessary time with his friend. Conveniently slip out to catch a chick flick with a girlfriend when you know that he is coming over to hang out at your house. Likewise, if you know that your husband would rather clean out every junk drawer in the house than spend time with one of your girls, make sure she's the one that you take to that chick flick.

And finally, Lesson Five of Family and Friends 101 is that all families have some drama. We're all special in our own way. I mean that in a very loving and sarcastic way. Every family has someone who is off their freakin' rocker. Every family has someone who talks too much, or eats too much, gossips too much, or drinks too much. There are secrets and rumors, and people who love to spend hours on the phone chatting about them. Don't be self-conscious or embarrassed about yours and don't judge him about his. And, most importantly, don't worry about what happens when you mix them all together. You are not responsible for the actions of your family nor is he for his family's behavior. Take that burden off of your shoulders and relax. When this aspect of family starts to freak you out, take a deep breath and remind yourself of Lesson Five. Again, it's that *ALL FAMILIES have some sort of drama.*

Things can get really sensitive when you start combining families and friends. The best thing that you can do is not worry. Remember that your marriage is an adjustment for your family and friends, too. Be respectful and considerate, and just know that there will be unexpected challenges along the way.

Don't Forget that Your Husband Is Number One Now

Now that you have started your new nuclear family, your husband fills that Number One spot. That doesn't mean that you love your family and friends any less, it simply means that your husband comes first.

Your parents, brothers and sisters, aunts and uncles, cousins and best friends are all people who love you very much. Most of them probably knew you before you knew your husband. So how did he jump past them to the top of your list? Because he married you, and aside from God, nothing and no one should ever come before you and your husband. Not your best friend from elementary school, not your cousin you spent summers with at the beach, and not even your mother who carried you nine long months in her womb. That doesn't mean that you love them any less, or that they are no longer important in your life. It simply means that they are not *numero uno* anymore, your husband is, and that can be a hard thing for your family and friends to accept.

Fortunately, there are things that you can do to make it easier for all of you.

1. NEVER MAKE YOUR FRIENDS AND FAMILY FEEL LIKE THEY ARE ANY LESS IMPORTANT TO YOU NOW. Just because your husband comes first doesn't mean that you have to advertise it. It's necessary for you to understand the level of commitment that you made to your husband, but it's not necessary for you to broadcast it.

2. NEVER ALLOW YOURSELF TO BE IN A POSITION TO HAVE TO CHOOSE BETWEEN YOUR FAMILY AND YOUR HUSBAND. You're not stranded on a desert island where you can only pick one person to stay. You love them all and you should continue to have relationships with everyone.

3. Never forget where you came from, and who was there for you before you met and married your new Number One. Maintaining relationships outside of your marriage is necessary for you as an individual. One is the loneliest number if you don't have two, three, four and five to balance it out.

Don't Expect to Hate Your Mother-In-Law

Don't expect your in-laws to be awful people. That's an old stereotype that can cause problems where there may not be any. Chances are you will probably like your in-laws, especially your mother-in-law, and believe it or not, grow to love them, too. If this is not the case, and your husband's family is the worst thing since polyester pants, you still need to make the effort to get along. These people raised the man you love. Do your best to respect them. Try to make things work for your husband's sake, for your marriage, and for your own peace of mind.

Be patient with your mother-in-law. You married her baby. Yes, her baby is a grown man complete with a grown man's mind, body and fully functioning sex drive, but to her, he's still her baby. And, believe it or not, *you* are the other woman. Not in a twisted unhealthy way, but in a natural way when a mother loves her son. She has always been the Number One woman in his life. Even through the high school honeys and the college co-eds.

Then came you.

Cut her some slack and let her get used to the situation. She might be loving and accepting from the start, or it might be rocky in the beginning. But before you tell all your girlfriends that she's worse than Jane Fonda in the movie *Monster-In-Law*, give her some time and space to adjust to the change.

A small and controllable amount of jealousy on her part is normal. Many of you will never even know she feels this way and some of you may feel the pain of her wrath constantly. If the latter is the case, don't try and go through it alone. Talk to your husband considerately. By this I mean that you should be mindful that it is his mother who is acting like the Wicked Witch of the West, so that you don't insult and alienate him. You need him to be your partner and help defuse the fireworks between the most important women in his life. If he's smart and likes peace in his life, he will work hard to cool things down. One upset woman is painful enough for him; no man wants his mother and his wife driving him crazy, especially at the same time.

Help him help you. He might not know what to do. If you want peace, it's your job to analyze the situation and figure out how everyone can compromise, especially how you and your husband can be happy. When you've figured it out, feed him the solution.

Easier said than done, right? Of course, but no one said this marriage thing was going to be easy. Try talking with your mother-in-law. Listen to what she says. Then, this time, step into her shoes. Be open to hearing and seeing the answers. Many times, they are so simple and right in front of your face.

Make sure that you're not harboring any jealous or competitive feelings toward her. She is the only other woman who can make your husband ask, "*How high?*" if she says, "*Jump.*" The temptation to compete with that can cause a lot of trouble. Let them have their special relationship and don't act silly over little things that only a mother can still do. Like when your husband has that one dish that only his mother can cook. He may eat yours, his favorite restaurant's, and even Martha Stewart's, but it will never be as good as his mama's. My advice is… don't cook it. For my husband, it's carrot cake, and after hearing him compare every slice he's ever tasted, I wouldn't dare put a piece in front of him to face the scrutiny, too. Suck it up and let her prepare it, especially since you can't win this one — his taste buds are pre-set to her recipe. Besides, it's something nice that his mom can still do for her son. Bow out gracefully and grab a fork.

Don't Be Surprised If Things Change between You and Your Single Friends

You shouldn't be surprised if some of your single girlfriends start to treat you a little differently now that you've tied the knot. Don't take it personally if your name suddenly gets dropped off the infamous ladies-night-out list. Some of your single friends will probably assume that you're hugged up with your husband, and that you would rather not go out. And quite honestly, some of them might be having a hard time dealing with the fact that you are married and they are not.

Again, communication is key here. Have a good ol' heart to heart with your closest girls. Meet them over a mocha latte and find out where their hearts and heads are. If they are supportive of your marriage and jealousy is not a factor, discuss how your new marital status will and most importantly won't change your friendships. Maybe you won't make it to every girls' night out, but simply let them know when you're ready and available.

Maybe all-night gossip sessions on the phone are out, but it's crucial that they know they can still call you at 3 a.m. if they need to. You're a woman and so are your friends. You know how women think. We like to be reassured, to know that we are still important and needed. Tell the ones that matter that they are, and even more so, show them.

Now, for the others who say everything is fine, but act like the world is ending, you may need to give them some extra time to adjust. Again, have a warm and fuzzy sit-down with these friends, too, and give them the opportunity to get used to your new situation. They might be genuinely happy for you and just genuinely miserable for themselves. You could be a painful reminder of what they don't have. That's understandable, but unfortunately it can put a serious strain on your relationship.

As our lives change, so do the dynamics of our friendships. Some will continue and adjust smoothly as if your husband has been there forever, and many who will never accept him may slowly fade out.

Both scenarios are normal and quite common. Don't worry, your true girlfriends will be there for you. Be patient as they adjust to their new roles, too. Some might be "everyday" girlfriends, some might be "two hour phone calls every six months" girlfriends, and some might be "I haven't seen you in a year but I never miss your birthday" girlfriends, and all of this is OK.

Family and Friends 101: Do's and Don'ts

DO UNDERSTAND THAT YOUR HUSBAND IS NOT HIS FAMILY. He is a part of them, but he should be his own person.

DO BE RESPECTFUL OF HIS PARENTS. Treat them with the same respect that you want your parents to be treated with.

DON'T BADMOUTH HIS FAMILY. Especially to him. He can talk about them like trash, but you can't. If you have to get it out, call your girlfriend and vent to her.

DO ALWAYS PRESENT A UNITED FRONT. Even if you've screamed until you can't talk anymore behind closed doors, always present a united front to your family.

DON'T GET IN THE MIDDLE OF HIS FAMILY FIGHTS IF THEY DON'T INVOLVE YOU. You're his wife, not his bodyguard. Let him handle his own family squabbles himself.

DO BE SUPPORTIVE DURING FAMILY SQUABBLES. He is your partner. While he needs to handle his own family disagreements himself, you should and can be supportive without getting directly involved.

DON'T LET YOUR FRIENDS AND FAMILY INVADE YOUR PRIVATE TIME. It is possible to see friends and family too much, even if you love them. Tactfully guard your couple time.

DO BE RESPECTFUL WHEN IT COMES TO OPPOSITE SEX FRIENDSHIPS. You shouldn't have to dump your male friends just because you made a trip to the altar. However, you should make sure that your husband knows your male amigos and that he is comfortable with your friendships. And the same goes for him and his female pals.

DON'T FREAK OUT IF HE KEEPS IN TOUCH WITH AN EX. If it's innocent (which it should be, since you just got married), an annual phone call is harmless.

DON'T TRY AND FORCE FAMILIES TOGETHER, ESPECIALLY IF THEY DON'T LIKE EACH OTHER. In this case, spend time with them separately and avoid the drama.

DON'T WORRY IF ARGUMENTS HAPPEN. Every family has arguments whether you're related by blood or marriage. Do your best to diffuse the situation, and then get over it.

DO COMPROMISE WHEN IT COMES TO HOLIDAYS. It's hard to choose which family to spend the holidays with. You can divide up holidays, alternate them, or when all fails stay home and make both families come to you.

DO CREATE YOUR OWN HOLIDAY TRADITIONS. Take a little from your family and a little from his, plus maybe something that you've seen someone else do and you've always wanted to try. It's a great time for new beginnings.

DO DECIDE WITH YOUR HUSBAND HOW LONG EACH FAMILY VISITS. Everything does not have to be even-steven. A two-week visit from his parents may fly by, but two weeks with your own mother might drive you insane.

DO LET HIS MOTHER COOK WHEN SHE COMES TO VISIT. Don't be territorial about your kitchen. Open it up to her and ask her to make your husband's favorite dish and yours too.

DON'T EVER MAKE HIM FEEL LIKE HE'S NOT AS SMART AS YOUR DAD. It's so easy to say, "*I'll ask my dad*," an authority you've looked to most of your life; but you should talk over important decisions with your husband now. It's OK to still look to your parents for guidance, just be considerate when you do it.

DON'T GET SUCKERED BY PARENTAL GUILT-TRIPPING. The guilt trips can happen so quickly that you won't know what hit you. Stand strong and make a decision that you and your hubby are happy with.

DO REMEMBER TO SEND HIS FAMILY BIRTHDAY AND HOLIDAY CARDS. Chances are he won't remember. His mom won't think her angel forgot, but that her new daughter-in-law did.

DO THINK LONG AND HARD BEFORE DECIDING TO HAVE A BABY. They're cute, adorable and fascinating, and they will change your life even more drastically than what you're going through now. Take it from someone who has two children; give yourselves a little time to build a foundation for your marriage and bank some sleep hours.

DO BE SUPPORTIVE IF HE ALREADY HAS CHILDREN. Whether you have a good relationship with these children or not, remember that you are an adult and they are children.

DON'T GET INTO A SPIRITUAL BATTLE WITH HIS FAMILY. Most people feel very strongly about their beliefs. Do not take part in a battle that no one can win; it will only start a family war.

Wives' Words

ABOUT IN-LAWS, FAMILY AND FRIENDS

"Family and friends are what builds a life and they are very important to your marriage. Don't let them be too involved but do involve them. Respect each other's friends, even the ones you don't necessarily like (unless they are just too too trifling)."
—ROBIN, MARRIED SIX YEARS

"It is not fair to make someone you love choose between people they love. Unless there is a harmful relationship in the bunch, then the more the merrier."
—RACHEL, MARRIED 12 YEARS

"Love your in-laws, family, and friends, but what happens at the house should stay at the house."
—MONICA, MARRIED THREE YEARS

"Don't bring them into your stuff. Your marriage is your business and yours alone." —ALLISON, MARRIED 12 YEARS

"If you have a mama's boy on your hands, and mama is giving advice about your household, your money, your child, and he always wants to follow mama's advice, you need to nip that business in the bud. Don't tell your family everything either because they will always remember the bad stuff you say about your spouse and will hold it against them. I also think it's important to have girlfriend time and for guys to have guy time. Your husband may be YOUR best friend, but he is not your girlfriend." —NANCY, MARRIED TWO YEARS

"Keep friends and family around that are supportive and positive."
—SHARON, MARRIED EIGHT YEARS

"Start from Day One creating loving boundaries. Keep some things sacred." —HOPE, MARRIED 14 YEARS

"If you marry into a relationship that involves children, you are taking on an awesome responsibility. You cannot go into the relationship thinking it's only about you and your spouse. If your spouse has children, well, when you get married, so do you. Also remove the words 'step' and 'half' from your vocabulary; it makes for a happier home!" —QUISA, MARRIED ONE YEAR

"In-laws — listen first, talk second. Friends — don't ignore them, we need friends. Make time to spend with friends."
—NDIDI, MARRIED SIX YEARS

"Be careful how you talk about your spouse's family."
—WANDA, MARRIED NINE YEARS

8

The Sports Fanatic

SURVIVING THE GAMES, THE BOYS, AND YOUR BEER-STAINED CARPET

Yikes! You married a sports fanatic. At times, it might seem like you married his boys, his favorite team, and a six-pack of beer, too. Sports are at the top of the list — behind money and sex — as one of the leading relationship wreckers. But don't despair; it doesn't have to be! If you're armed with some basic information and if you make a genuine effort to understand your husband's infatuation with sports, then you, too, can be married to a sports fanatic and survive to tell about it.

At the risk of stereotyping — OK, I'm stereotyping — sports to most men is like shopping to most women. It's exhilarating, emotional, addictive, and can drive your spouse absolutely crazy. Most husbands don't understand the thrill of a good shopping spree, especially when you hit an end-of-the-season sale. To them, our obsessive, compulsive behavior is downright scary. In turn, a playoff game with your husband's favorite team in contention for the national championship is just as intense to him.

Not all men love sports, and not all women are clueless about sports. But for those of you who are not athletically inclined and married a sports fanatic, no matter what his passion — basketball, football, golf and/or hockey — there are some things that you can know and do to keep a little sanity in your life.

First of all, you should know the basics about your husband's favorite sport. You don't have to go overboard and know how to call plays in the huddle, but you should know what a play and a huddle are.

If you married a sports man, then it's inevitable that he will tune into his favorite one constantly during its season. What sport he loves will determine how often he is camped out in front of the television. Basketball, for instance, is played several days throughout the week, while football is a one-game-a-week sport. Now, cable and satellite TV have sports packages like NBA League Pass and NFL Sunday Ticket where your husband can buy access to every game. Yes, *every* game. Not just what is airing on local television, but what is happening hundreds of miles away, too. For those of you who don't know, that's a lot of freakin' games.

You have a few choices on how to handle this. You can bitch, complain, moan, and fight, and be the wife that all his friends are glad they *didn't* marry; or you can be a cool wife and relax, accept it, be nice, and probably get your way more often because you let him enjoy his necessary dose of testosterone.

If you opt for the cool wife role, I'm very proud of you. It's really easy to be a cool wife once you decide to do it. If you don't like football, then make Sunday afternoons your time to go shopping, visit the spa, or hang out with the ladies. Take advantage of the time that he's glued to the television set to do something special *for you*.

Or you can learn about his favorite game. Watch it with him, but save your questions for during the commercials. You're not a cool wife if you spend the whole game asking, *"What's this? What's that? What's this?"* Instead you'll be the annoying one. If you really want to be daring and take your coolness to the next level, pick him up some game snacks — peanuts, chips, buffalo wings, beer — when you know he's having the boys over, and then disappear for the rest of the day. That fancy move will score you big points.

And for the beer-stained carpet, arm your husband with some handheld spray cleaner, a wet rag, and explicit instructions. Yes, you can tolerate his rowdy friends. You are fine with an afternoon of first downs, instant replays, and two-point conversions. You can even deal with a messy kitchen (hint, hint — give him plenty of plastic ware and point him toward the garbage). However, the lasting stench of a beer-stained carpet is where you draw the line.

Do Know the Signs of a Sports Fanatic

If you married a man who likes sports, it is very important to know what you're dealing with so that you can react, or even more so, prepare yourself accordingly. Is he an "over-the-top, might spend the rent money on tickets to see his favorite team" kind of guy? Or does he like sports but doesn't plan his schedule around game times and watches them only if he has nothing else to do? And yes, men will plan their schedule around important games. Napoleon, an ex-college football player himself, did give me free rein in planning our wedding except that it could absolutely not be during football season, especially on the Saturday that Florida State plays Florida.

The depth of your husband's intensity about sports will dictate your course of actions. If he is more manageable, you might not like it, but could go with the flow and be glad he's not painting his face his team colors and spouting off statistics at every meal. If he *is* doing those things, make sure to utilize the Four C's — communication, compromise, creativity and commitment (see Chapter Two).

Chances are that you knew about his sports obsession before you married him. Now that you are husband and wife and live together, it's totally appropriate to set some boundaries so that he can still enjoy his love of sports and you can choose to join him or not.

Below are ten signs of a sports fanatic. If you recognize any of these in your husband, don't panic. Just prepare yourself, your house, and your husband with some guidelines to make sure that March madness doesn't cause mayhem in your marriage.

Ten signs of a sports fanatic...

Your husband's score is determined by how many signs apply to him. Give your hubby one point for every behavior that applies.

1. **He watches ESPN's *SportsCenter* more than three times in a row.** *SportsCenter*, a daily sports news show, often re-airs the same show several times a day until the next one is produced. It's like watching the same *Entertainment Tonight* more than once.

2. **He listens to sports radio every time he's in the car and thinks the "2 Live Stews" should run for political office.** The "2 Live Stews" are two brothers who have one of the most popular nationally syndicated sports talk shows in the country. Think *The View* for men — hot topics and all.

3. **He's superstitious and has to wear his team's jersey, baseball hat, underwear, socks or some sort of paraphernalia while watching the game.** He'll even pull it out of the dirty laundry if it's not clean. OK, I'm not telling on Napoleon here, but let's just say I can vouch for this one from firsthand experience.

4. **If his team loses, you can pretty much forget the romantic dinner that you planned for later.** His mood is ruined as if he missed the game-winning field goal himself.

5. **His idea of the perfect trip is traveling across country by plane, train or automobile to tailgate (enjoy barbecue and beer) in the parking lot of the stadium where his favorite team plays even if he doesn't have tickets to go in and see the game.** Being in the parking lot is enough for him.

6. **He really can't understand why his team's bean bag, blanket, throw pillows, lamp and football-shaped clock do not go with the decor of your living room.** Refer to the Living Together chapter; this is exactly why every man should have his own space in your home.

7. He can't remember your birth date, how old his mother is, or to pick up the dry-cleaning on his way home from work, but he can tell you who won the 1982 Super Bowl (the San Francisco 49ers) and recite all of the game statistics, including who quarterbacked, how many yards he threw for, what the defense did, and give you an announcer's style descriptive play-by-play of the entire game.

8. **He thinks NASCAR would be a great name for your first child.** Boy or girl.

9. **He seriously suggested borrowing against his 401k or taking out a second mortgage on your house to buy one season ticket for his favorite team.** *One.* That means even if you want to, you don't get to go.

10. **He enters every "biggest fan" contest dying for the opportunity to live out his childhood (and grownman) fantasies** — stepping into the batter's box and slugging a homerun out of the ballpark; throwing that halftime, half-court basketball shot in front of thousands of screaming fans; or receiving a kick and returning it the entire length of the football field.

See how your husband scores

1-3 IS MILD — Consider yourself lucky and go with the flow.

4-7, MODERATE — It can get pretty intense, but be patient and set parameters. Give his favorite sport a try or take advantage of the time to do something for yourself.

8 OR MORE, MANIAC — Your man has the potential to get out of control. You and your husband need to come up with "game rules" to keep him and *you* from going crazy. If you two can't communicate and compromise effectively — in the off season so that he can be objective — seek a referee or professional help, and pray that his team has a winning season.

Do Take Advantage of the Time

As I will keep saying throughout the chapter, if you are not a sports lover, take advantage of the time that he is enjoying sports to enjoy something yourself. Do not focus on his behavior and spend excessive negative energy nagging, yes I said it, nagging him about sports (unless he is a maniac and then you need to seriously address it). He's having a good time enjoying something that he likes. Either enjoy it with him or find something that you enjoy, too.

Yes, you are a couple now, but you still need to nurture your individuality. It is OK and encouraged to have some separate interests of your own. Be one with yourself. Discover a passion that is hidden in the depths of your soul. And if that's too deep for you, grab your purse and a girlfriend and go shopping. See a movie, get a massage, go to a play, read a book, catch up on some sleep. Do something (except bitch at him) that will make you happy, too.

Do Take Fantasy Sports Seriously

Most men who play fantasy sports take them seriously. It's an opportunity for them to feel directly involved with professional or collegiate sports. And there can be money at stake, possibly hundreds of dollars that they can win. Sometimes they need to pay to get in the league.

What are fantasy sports? And isn't the real thing enough? You would think so, but apparently not. A fantasy sport, or league, is a group of virtual teams or players — depending on the sport — who compete against each other based on real sports statistics. Your husband is the owner or manager of one of these virtual teams that is created by using real players and statistics from real professional games.

There are fantasy leagues for just about every popular sport including basketball, baseball, golf, NASCAR, hockey, and soccer. However, for the sake of simplicity, I'll use football as a reference.

Without going too deep into the process (I don't want to confuse or lose anyone who is not that sports savvy), the following are the key points that you need to know when it comes to fantasy leagues:

1. **They can cost money to play.** Hey, anything that your husband does that can take dollars out of the bank account deserves a little attention.

2. **They can win him money.** One of the reasons he takes it so seriously, aside from his ingrained masculine competitiveness, is that he could win — depending on the league — a nice chunk of money.

3. **This is big business in the sports world.** Millions of people play fantasy sports, and there are many websites, magazines, and even television shows dedicated to fantasy sports. As we continue to live in a tech-

nologically advanced world, fantasy leagues will continue to grow.

4. **He really is participating in an owners/coaches meeting and draft to kick off the season.** It's just virtual. This can be done via a conference call, in person at someone's house, or in a bar. The purpose of this initial meeting is to set up his team by choosing and trading players.

5. **They are having fun while doing this.** They take it seriously, but it is sports. You can bet on some beer and chicken wings being consumed at this "very important" event.

6. **They use players from the actual league.** Their fantasy team accumulates points based on the statistics or how a particular player or players perform in the real NFL game that day. In football, your husband's fantasy team will have players from several different teams in the NFL.

7. **Your husband may be cheering for his favorite NFL team to win, while also cheering for a player on the opposing team, too.** It can get a little confusing if you are watching this obvious conflict of interest, but it's simple. He wants his favorite team to win "in real life" but wants the player on his fantasy team who happens to be playing against his favorite real team to play well, too.

The bottom line with fantasy sports is: *don't let the word fantasy fool you!* Even though your husband and his friends may be playing a virtual game, whenever there may be money, time or emotion involved, it's real.

Do Know When Key Sporting Events Happen

Create a calendar of sporting events that your husband likes to watch. It will make living with him much easier. You don't need the exact dates for everything, but be prepared and know when the big events are happening. If your husband is a football fan, you don't want to plan a romantic dinner the night of the Super Bowl.

To get you started, here's a general timeline of when several major sporting events happen. You should ask your husband or look on the internet for details on his favorite sports. And remember, living with a sports fanatic doesn't have to be a painful, dreaded thing; it all depends on how you play the game.

January
College football bowl games, New Year's Day (and the following week)
NFL Playoffs begin, football

February
The Super Bowl, football
NBA All Star Game, basketball
NFL Pro Bowl, football
Daytona 500, NASCAR racing

March
March Madness, college basketball playoffs
MLB Spring Training, baseball

April
MLB Season begins, baseball
The Masters, golf tournament
NFL Draft, football

May
Indianapolis 500, car racing
French Open begins, tennis

June
US Open, golf tournament
Wimbledon begins, tennis
NBA Finals, basketball
NBA Draft, basketball
NHL Stanley Cup Finals, hockey

July
MLB All-Star Game, baseball
British Open, golf tournament

August
PGA Championship, golf tournament
NFL Preseason, football
US Open begins, tennis

September
College football begins
NFL season begins, football

October
NBA preseason, basketball

NBA season begins, basketball
MLB World Series, baseball

November
College basketball begins
Football and basketball games, Thanksgiving Day

December
Football and basketball games, Christmas Day
College football bowl games begin

The Sports Fanatic: Do's and Don'ts

DO KNOW THE BASICS ABOUT YOUR HUSBAND'S FA-
VORITE SPORTS. Football has a quarterback, basketball
a point guard, baseball a pitcher… get the point?

DO WATCH THE GAME WITH HIM. Give it a try. You might
like it, too. If nothing else, it's nice to watch those good-
looking bodies running around glistening with sweat.

DON'T TRY TO BE ONE OF THE BOYS. There are times
when men just want to hang out and watch the game with
other men. It doesn't matter if you love the sport, too; it's
a male bonding thing. So, if it's a "guys only" event, don't
intrude.

DO ASK HIM TO TEACH YOU A LITTLE BIT ABOUT THE
GAME. He'll probably appreciate your interest.

DON'T ASK HIM TO TEACH YOU ABOUT THE GAME
DURING THE SUPER BOWL, NBA FINALS, OR THE
18TH HOLE OF THE MASTERS. He probably won't appreciate your interest.

DON'T TRY AND HAVE A SERIOUS CONVERSATION WITH HIM WHILE HE IS WATCHING A GAME. It doesn't work. Even if he acts like he's paying attention to you, he probably isn't.

DON'T TEASE HIM RIGHT AWAY IF HIS TEAM LOSES A BIG GAME. Some men take it as personally as if they missed the game-winning pass themselves.

DO KNOW THAT ESPN's *SPORTSCENTER* REPEATS ITSELF SEVERAL TIMES A DAY. Bear through it once, maybe twice, but don't miss *Oprah* over it.

DON'T GIVE HIM GRIEF ABOUT BUYING THE *SPORTS ILLUSTRATED* SWIMSUIT ISSUE. Suck it up, and let it go. It's only once a year.

DO CREATE YOUR OWN SWIMSUIT ISSUE. If it bothers you that much, take your own sexy pictures — or better yet, model your bikini in person.

DO BE PREPARED FOR GAMES ON HOLIDAYS. Thanksgiving, Christmas, and New Year's Day are all big game days for basketball and football.

DO GIVE HIM TEAM PARAPHERNALIA FOR GIFTS. It makes birthday and holiday shopping easy. If he is a true fan, he can't have enough T-shirts, hats, sweatshirts or even underwear with his team logo on it.

DO ATTEND HIS GAMES IF HE PLAYS ON ANY RECREATIONAL TEAMS. Don't make fun of your husband's attempt to recapture his youth by playing flag football on Saturday afternoons. Pack a picnic basket and go cheer him on in the park.

DON'T BE AFRAID TO GET INVOLVED. You've heard the famous saying, "If you can't beat them, join them." Stay active together and play on a co-ed team with your husband.

DO DRESS CASUALLY IF HE IS TAKING YOU TO A GAME. Most sporting events are very casual… jeans, shorts, and T-shirts are all appropriate for basketball, football, baseball, and hockey games.

DON'T CHEER IF YOU DON'T KNOW WHO OR WHAT YOU ARE CHEERING FOR. Sports fans take their teams and their games very seriously. You don't want to start a riot by cheering for the wrong team or the wrong player.

DON'T TALK TOO MUCH. Light conversation is good at a game. Don't bring up cleaning out the garage or the gossip your coworker told you at work.

DO RELAX AND HAVE FUN. You're spending time with your husband, and you're a cool wife… remember?

Wives' Words

ABOUT MARRYING A SPORTS FANATIC

"Deal with it (unless it is truly affecting your relationship). This is what they do. This is how they bond."

—ROBIN, MARRIED SIX YEARS

"You can do one of two things: get into sports, or go upstairs and watch the Food Network while he's watching the game. Guys like girls who are hot, drink beer, and like sports. So I'm working on it. Two out of three (hot and I drink beer) ain't bad."

—NANCY, MARRIED TWO YEARS

"Understand and know that this definitely will not change. Either fight it and be miserable — or embrace and travel with him to out-of-town games."

—CHERYL, MARRIED FIVE YEARS

"Let the man enjoy his sports. That frees you up to hang with the girls unless you enjoy sports too."

—MONICA, MARRIED THREE YEARS

"All I can say is have patience and if you can't beat 'em, join 'em. Sit and watch the games with him at least every now and then. If that doesn't work, put a teddy on if need be and give him a halftime show he'll never forget."

—ALLISON, MARRIED 12 YEARS

"Throw on a jersey and join in on the fun."

—SHARON, MARRIED EIGHT YEARS

"I love sports, especially football. We have sports in common. Oddly enough, he has learned to love sports even more since we got married."

—JEN, MARRIED FOUR MONTHS

"I am a 'golf widow' and the only thing I can say is 'if you can't beat 'em, join 'em.' We recently went on a vacation, and my husband asked me to go with him to play golf (I nearly had a heart attack that he asked me). I ended up going with him, and we have not connected like that in a long time. He opened up to me... It was just great, because I got to see him doing something he really loves, and he shared it with me."

—HOPE, MARRIED 14 YEARS

"There is room for both sports and you."

—NDIDI, MARRIED SIX YEARS

9

Just for Him

HOW TO LOVE HER, HUMOR HER, AND
STAY OUT OF THE DOGHOUSE

OK, husbands, I'm a realist. I know that reading a new-lywed book is probably not how you would choose to spend your time, but here you are. Under duress, I'm sure, but you're here nonetheless. Your wife couldn't put this book down and has been constantly yelling bits and pieces out to you. Now she's gone over the edge and has actually handed it to you to read. *"Honey, you've got to see this! It's a chapter just for you!"*

So what do you do? Tell her, *"No!"* and spend the night in the doghouse? Or read it reluctantly and possibly learn something? (If you don't know which to do, you definite-ly need to read this chapter and possibly the entire book.) You're a husband now, and sometimes — OK, a lot of the time — husbands need to do things to humor their wives. Humoring your wife is not selling out, being whipped, or be-ing a punk. I like to think of it more as keeping the peace and a necessary thing for a husband to do to keep his wife happy, his marriage growing, and his own peace of mind.

For example, your wife comes home from the beauty salon, gives you a kiss, and stands there staring at you impatiently. What is she waiting for? For you to tell her that her hair looks nice! It doesn't matter if it does. Your wife could look like she just took a ride in a convertible through a windstorm, but she still wants to hear it looks nice. Now I'm not advising you to lie to your wife, but *sometimes* you have to humor her. You see, if you tell her that her hair looks bad, you undoubtedly set yourself up for an intense round of questioning. "*Do you really think it looks bad? Why does it look bad? I'm ugly. Do you think I'm ugly?*" and then come the tears. Husbands, do you really want to go there? Trust me, if it looks bad, she already knows it, and she doesn't want to hear it from you. And don't forget to look at her first before you tell her that her hair looks nice. Yes, only once did my husband make that mistake. The fact that he said something without even looking was worse than no compliment at all.

Being a husband is new to you, and marriage doesn't come with an instruction manual like a computer or a flat-screen TV. It can be confusing, challenging, overwhelming and downright scary. But it doesn't have to be if you communicate and compromise with your wife, if you're creative (that's where a little humoring comes in), and if you stay committed to your marriage.

Oh, and a few other things wouldn't hurt either. Like buying her flowers for no reason, or cuddling with her in bed instead of rolling over and falling asleep. We wives know that most husbands don't particularly care about these things, but that's what makes it even more special when you do them.

If you take the time to look through the rest of this book, you will see that I've given your wife many Do's and Don'ts that will essentially hook you up. I've told her not to bother you while you're watching the game, not to nag you about leaving your pants on the floor, and most importantly, to make sure she stays a hot, sexy chick. So read on, take notes, and try to find it in your heart to hook her up, too. Or, at least, humor her.

But before you go to the other chapters, I have some Do's and Don'ts just for the husbands for you to check out. Plus some words of advice from other wives.

Just for Him: Do's and Don'ts

DO TELL HER SHE IS BEAUTIFUL. Not only when she's dressed up to go out, but when she's lying around the house with no makeup on simply looking beautiful.

DON'T EVER FORGET HER BIRTHDAY — EVER. It could take months to recover from that one.

DO WEAR YOUR WEDDING RING. It's a symbol of your love and commitment. Wear it proudly.

DO TAKE CARE OF HER WHEN SHE'S SICK. Cater to your wife the same way she caters to you when you're sick.

DON'T ANSWER "YES, DEAR" UNLESS YOU HEARD WHAT SHE IS ASKING. And don't get mad at your wife when you've said, "Yes" to something that you don't really want to do.

DON'T WATCH TELEVISION WHEN YOUR WIFE IS TRY-
ING TO HAVE A SERIOUS CONVERSATION WITH YOU.
It only makes her more upset which ends up being worse
for you.

DO LET HER KNOW YOUR NEEDS. Especially when you
need your "man" time. If you don't tell her, she won't
know, and you won't get it.

DON'T EVER TELL A WOMAN WHO IS ACTING BITCHY
THAT SHE MUST BE HAVING HER PERIOD. Especially
if she is.

DON'T LET YOUR EGO STOP YOU FROM ASKING FOR
DRIVING DIRECTIONS WHEN SHE'S WITH YOU. It's
a woman's pet peeve. If you want to drive around lost
for hours by yourself, fine. But don't do it with her in the
car.

DO COMPLIMENT YOUR WIFE WHEN SHE COOKS YOU A
NICE MEAL. Let her know that you appreciate the time
she took to cook for you.

DO BE HONEST IF SHE COOKS SOMETHING THAT YOU
DON'T CARE FOR. Just be sensitive. Don't say, "It's nasty."
Try… "It's OK, but I love when you make…"

DO COOK FOR HER. Men who can cook are sexy.

DON'T EXPECT HER TO BE YOUR MOTHER. Sometimes
you hate when she acts like she's your mother, but some-

times you expect some mothering. She's not your mother, so don't expect her to act like it.

Don't check out other women when you're with her. Just because you're married doesn't mean you're blind. However, don't be disrespectful and look at other women when your wife is there to see you do it. Instant ticket to the doghouse.

Do know that romance is more than flowers and candy. It's looking into her eyes when you're talking, it's cuddling on the couch, it's opening the car door for her…

Do know what romance means to her. Ask her what makes her melt, and listen when she tells you.

Do know that you can give your wife flowers without a reason. That makes getting them ten million times better.

Don't think foreplay starts when you're about to have sex. It has a lot to do with how you treat her throughout the day.

Don't fart in bed and think you're going to get some sex. There's a time limit that has to elapse between disgusting behavior and sexual behavior. You just turned your bedroom into a locker room, now you have to do something to get her back in the mood.

Wives' Words

JUST FOR HIM

"When your wife is venting, don't try to fix her problems — simply listen. That's all she wants... really. If she wants your advice, she will ask you for it."
—NDIDI, MARRIED SIX YEARS

"Chivalry is not dead! No matter how liberated she is, open the door for your woman... surprise her with flowers from time to time for no apparent reason... make her feel like a woman!"
—NOELLE, MARRIED 10 YEARS

"Communicate; we cannot read minds. Tell her you love her. Tell her how she looks, before she asks. Set up the chores early in the relationship, so that there aren't any questions. So when the bathroom isn't cleaned, you know who to blame. Choose your battles wisely. Some may not be worth the fight. And try and think before you speak in a heated discussion. Life is short and we are not promised tomorrow."
—BOBETTE, MARRIED 10 YEARS

"Listen! Listen! Listen! If you can do that one thing, keeping your wife's feelings in mind, everything will be alright."
—HOPE, MARRIED 14 YEARS

"Being completely honest and open with your wife is probably one of the sexiest things that you could for your wife."
—CHERYL, MARRIED FIVE YEARS

"Your wife has to come first, understand that when you get married you become one. YOU ARE NOT DATING! Find some space in your house where you can unwind when she gets on your nerves. Also, tell her you love her at least once a week. Don't forget to spice it up in the bedroom; get some hot PJs and be creative in bed. When your married sex should be even hotter, you've got to pull out some new tricks; and if you don't know any, learn some!"

—WANDA, MARRIED NINE YEARS

"My advice to guys is regarding sex and how to get more... Try giving compliments and cuddles without sex. Women like to feel loved; it makes us feel sexy and then great sex abounds."

—RACHEL, MARRIED 12 YEARS

"Even after you marry, you must remain friends. Don't think about leaving when times get hard. Hang in there and remember why you got married."

—TRACEY, MARRIED 14 YEARS

Afterword

365 Days Later

BREAK OUT THE BUBBLY AND CELEBRATE! IT'S YOUR ANNIVERSARY!

Happy Anniversary! You did it! You survived the first year of marriage, and I hope you're even more in love with your husband than you were 365 days ago. You've accomplished so much during this past year. Being married is really hard work and you should be proud of all you've done.

During the past year. you've had a chance to apply my more than 225 Do's and Don'ts to help yourself do more than survive your marriage, but thrive in it, too. Now I have a few anniversary Do's and Don'ts to help you celebrate the end of your first year and the beginning of many more to come.

Do Make Sure You Celebrate

Your first anniversary is one of the most special and exciting days of your marriage; make sure you make a big deal of it. Talk to your husband and decide on making it a special day that will be sentimental to you both. Share an intimate dinner at your reception site or recreate your wedding menu in the privacy of your own home. Take out your wedding trinkets — napkins, toasting glasses, candles — and set the dinner table as it looked the night you became husband and wife. If you really want to get creative and a little freaky, put on your wedding dress — remember how much fun you two had taking it off?

Or you may want to ditch last year's wedding duds and pick up a sexy strapless dress and start anew in Year Two. Perhaps casual couple time is more your cup of tea. Just like most of the advice in this book, there is no right or wrong way to celebrate your first year of marriage — just make sure you do something!

Some couples take a vacation every year to acknowledge their anniversary, while others renew their vows. The things that you and your husband can do to celebrate your union are endless. Put your creative veil back on and make it a night to remember.

However you decide to honor your special day, make sure that you try to incorporate these three important things:

1. REMINISCE ABOUT THE PAST. Celebrate all the struggles you've overcome and all of the good times you've had.

2. ENJOY THE MOMENT. Create new memories and start your own anniversary tradition.

3. LOOK TO THE FUTURE. Break out the bubbly and toast to all the anniversaries still to come. Here's to fifty more!

365 Days Later: Do's and Don'ts

DO ACKNOWLEDGE WHAT A GREAT JOB YOU BOTH HAVE DONE DURING YOUR FIRST YEAR OF MARRIAGE. Recognize the effort you both have put into building a happy life together.

DON'T EXPECT YOUR RELATIONSHIP TO BE PERFECT IN ONE YEAR. First of all, nothing is ever perfect, and secondly, it takes years to build a great marriage. Just do everything you can to start out on the right foot.

DO PLAN FOR YOUR SECOND YEAR. You probably had just as many, if not more, successes during your first year than you had mistakes. For Year Two, identify and build on the things you're happy with and make a conscious effort to change the things you didn't like.

DO TELL EVERYONE IT'S YOUR ANNIVERSARY. Your first year of marriage is special and a big accomplishment. Tell the world you did it.

DON'T EXPECT EVERYONE TO FUSS OVER YOU LIKE THEY DID FOR YOUR WEDDING. Except for your parents, who are probably as thrilled as you are about your successful first year, most people will congratulate you and move on.

DO REMINISCE ABOUT YOUR WEDDING DAY. Watch the video, take out the photo album, and remember the ups and downs of your wonderful day.

Do look forward to many more. This is the first of many anniversaries to come. Picture yourselves fifty years from now and work hard to get there.

Now it's time to finish this book and begin creating the rest of your wonderful, loving, sometimes scary but strong marriage together. Take a deep breath, enjoy and thrive.

Wives' Words

WHAT IS THE BEST THING THAT HAPPENED TO YOU DURING YOUR FIRST YEAR?

"We became better friends. A lot of our relationship had been long distance, so the uninterrupted time together was invaluable."

—ROBIN, MARRIED SIX YEARS

"We built a solid framework for marriage and got pregnant!"

—NDIDI, MARRIED SIX YEARS

"Becoming part of Rick's family."

—NANCY, MARRIED TWO YEARS

"The best thing that happened was that my husband and I began to learn more about God. We started attending Bible Study and Church on a weekly basis and started understanding what role each of us played in our marriage."

—MONICA, MARRIED THREE YEARS

"We worked together a lot and had fun."

—RHONDA, MARRIED 20 YEARS

"Great wedding, great honeymoon in Mexico, friends and family, and celebrations."

—SHARON, MARRIED EIGHT YEARS

"The best thing that's happened to me, aside from the conception of our first child, is seeing the change and maturation in myself. Marriage comes with a new feeling of responsibility to nurture and protect my 'new' family, as small as it may be."

—JENNIFER, MARRIED FOUR MONTHS

"We got to make love whenever we wanted to, and a whole lot."
—HOPE, MARRIED 14 YEARS

"We were forced to spend more time together. Because our careers are demanding, we didn't make time to take a honeymoon, therefore we have made a commitment to have 'couple' time at least once a week."
—QUISA, MARRIED ONE YEAR

"I realized that my husband loved me and was trying as hard as I was to learn how to be a good mate."
—RACHEL, MARRIED 12 YEARS

Wifey Reading & Resources

As much as I would like to think that my voice is the only one that needs to be heard, I do realize that I am the *only* person who would feel that way. So I have compiled a brief list of resources that might be helpful to you, your husband and your peace of mind. As I said in my introduction, there are no rights and wrongs here, just many different resources and many different views. In fact, there are too many to include here, so I invite you to visit my website, www.AskWifey. com for a more comprehensive list.

I urge you to explore these and other resources, while keeping two things in mind — be open to learning something that you didn't know and be smart enough to ignore something that doesn't work for you. Your marriage will be better for it!

BOOKS

The Nest Newlywed Handbook: An Owner's Manual for Modern Married Life by Carley Roney

The Don't Sweat Guide for Newlyweds: Finding What Matters Most in the First Year by Richard Carlson

What No One Tells the Bride by Marg Stark

Crib Notes for the First Year of Marriage: A Survival Guide for Newlyweds by Everett D. Morier

Lies at the Altar: The Truth about Great Marriages by Robin
L. Smith

*The Conscious Bride: Women Unveil Their True Feelings
About Getting Hitched* by Sheryl Paul

*The Meaning of Wife: A Provocative Look at Women and
Marriage in the Twenty-first Century* by Anne Kingston

*Chicken Soup for the Bride's Soul: Stories of Love, Laughter
and Commitment to Last a Lifetime* by Jack Canfield,
Mark Victor Hansen, Maria Nickless and Gina
Romanello

*The New Rules of Marriage: What You Need to Know to Make
Love Work* by Terrence Real

*Men Are from Mars, Women Are from Venus: The Classic
Guide to Understanding the Opposite Sex* by John Gray

*The Bitch in the House: 26 Women Tell the Truth About Sex,
Solitude, Work, Motherhood and Marriage* by Cathi
Hanauer

The Proper Care and Feeding of Marriage by Dr. Laura
Schlessinger

*The Surrendered Wife: A Practical Guide to Finding Intimacy,
Passion and Peace with Your Man* by Laura Doyle

The Money Book for the Young, Fabulous & Broke by Suze
Orman

The Road to Wealth: A Comprehensive Guide to Your Money
by Suze Orman

*For Richer Not Poorer: The Newlywed's Financial Survival
Guide* by Deborah Wilburn

Get Your Own Damn Beer, I'm Watching the Game!: A Woman's Guide to Loving Pro Football by Holly Robinson Peete, Daniel Paisner and Marcus Allen

Rachel Ray 2, 4, 6, 8: Great Meals for Couples or Crowds by Rachel Ray

Your Money and Your Man: How You and Prince Charming Can Spend Well and Live Rich by Michelle Singletary

Rich Dad, Poor Dad by Robert T. Kiyosaki and Sharon L. Lechter, C.P.A.

Rich Woman: A Book on Investing for Women — Because I Hate Being Told What to Do! by Kim Kiyosaki

Make Money, Not Excuses: Wake Up, Take Charge and Overcome Your Financial Fears Forever by Jean Chatzky

WEBSITES

www.thenest.com

www.myfico.com

www.experian.com

www.transunion.com

www.equifax.com

www.socialsecurity.gov

www.emilypost.com

www.espn.go.com

http://games.espn.go.com (fantasy sports)

http://sportsline.com/fantasy (fantasy sports)

About Wifey

Lorraine Sanabria Robertson is the Author of *Help! I'm a Newlywed... What Do I Do Now? Wife-Saving Advice Every New Bride Must Know to Survive the First Year of Marriage* (30 Miles Media, Inc.) and the creator of AskWifey.com. She is a nationally published freelance writer and successful public relations executive. Her work has appeared in various publications including *Teen People, Upscale*, and *Heart & Soul* magazines. With more than 13 years of entertainment industry experience, this former Director of Publicity for LaFace Records has contributed to the success of several superstar recording artists including Usher, OutKast, TLC, and Toni Braxton. She also served as Assistant Director of Public Relations for Spelman College, one of the most prestigious women's colleges in the world. Happily married for eight years, Lorraine currently lives in Atlanta with her husband, Napoleon, and their children, Miles and Milan. Her life-changing wedding was featured on The Learning Channel's popular television show, *A Wedding Story*.